What a Woman Is Worth

Tamára Lunardo, Editor

Thanks
so much,
Abigail!
— Sarah
Moon

CivitasPress

Publishing inspiring and redemptive ideas.

2

ISBN # 978-0615956633

Published by Civitas Press, LLC

San Jose, CA

www.civitaspress.com

To my children — because you're worth it all.

Endorsements

"A powerful, moving read, 'What a Woman Is Worth' brings together an all-star cast of today's best storytellers to tackle some of the biggest, most complicated questions of the heart with unusual bravery and grace. The writing is sharp, funny, colorful, and raw, and the diversity of perspectives represented in this collection brings womanhood--in all its contradictions and shades--to life. It's a celebration of what we all have in common, and it's beautiful." — Rachel Held Evans, author of A Year of Biblical Womanhood

"The question of our worth lies at the root of so many things that hold us back in shame, fear, or doubt. This book is a brave 'I'll go first,' inspiring all who read it to take important steps forward into freedom." — Kristen Howerton, Professor of Psychology, Vanguard University and author of RageAgainsttheMinivan.com

"*What a Woman Is Worth* is a powerful collection of voices finding their home. Through words, these women link arms and make the powerful statement that our worth will be found in the whispering of our stories. The time for silence is over, and Lunardo does a beautiful job collecting and guiding these voices into song." — Elora Ramirez, author of *Every Shattered Thing*

"A must-read for any parent concerned about how girls receive, internalize, and manifest the myriad subtle familial and societal messages about a woman's worth." — Cymande Baxter-Rogers, ARNP

"*What a Woman Is Worth* is an engaging series of essays. Challenging, convicting, and artfully rendered, the collection of voices offers not only unique perspectives on what it is to be a woman but also how different women come to terms with defining womanhood -- for themselves and for others." — Preston Yancey, author of *Tables in the Wilderness: A Memoir of God Found, Lost, and Found Again* (Zondervan)

"Powerful, compelling, and sometimes heartbreaking, *What a Woman Is Worth* reminded me of the destructive narrative often force-fed to women in our culture." — Shawn Smucker, author of *Refuse To Drown*

Acknowledgements

This book has been a tremendous labor of love, tears, and gnashing of teeth, and it would not have come to fruition without the help of so many good people:

Jonathan Brink, my publisher, who believed in my story from the start and pushed me to the finish; Luke, Natalie, Mia, Tessa, and Scarlett, who sacrificed their mommy time because they love their mommy; Bryan, who made a place for me to write when I could and made a place for me to heal when I couldn't; my family—especially Mom, Dad, and Casey—who never gave up on me or my project even when I repeatedly doubted both; Lauren Relyea, and Brownie Troop 456 and their leaders, who took care of my youngest daughters so that I could take care with people's stories; Stephen Addcox, who lent a careful eye and thoughtful heart to the difficult selection process; Sarah West, who baked me scones and brownies so that I'd stay seated at my computer just a little longer; Trish Baumann and Renee Ronika who reminded me of my calling when I couldn't hear it; the fiercely loyal readers of my blog, Tamára Out Loud, who lifted me with encouragement and covered me with prayer; the scores of brave people who submitted their stories, and the thirty women whose hearts are ultimately bared here for the benefit of others; and the God who has been with me every moment, even when I didn't feel it or believe it, just because He thought I was worth it.

Contents

Part 4: Am I Good Enough?
Stories of Expectations and Pressures

Part 5: Am I Whole? Stories of Faith

Introduction

It began with a question even before I was born.

Just a swell in my mother's belly, I was punched by a hand that was meant to hold me. I was not even here yet, and already my worth was in doubt. As I grew, so would the question, and it would gnaw at me — unarticulated, insidious, and damning.

My world told me stories of my worth, and I believed them. So I lived into what I believed, which is to say, I did not live fully well.

Still, story was what I knew; how, in rare moments, I lived; how I could still, in some small way, be the truest me. So I let out a bit of my story into the online pages of a site for which I write: A Deeper Story. I knew I was searching for a deeper story than the one my world had been telling me, and so I broke and I bared and I finally asked out loud the hardest question of my life a blog post entitled, *What's a Girl Worth*?

> I was 13– Excited to be out late at Denny's with my friends, talking and laughing, effervescent, carefree. He was much older, at least in his 30s, but he zeroed in on me. He leered, scruffy face so close, stinking drunk, and he loud-whispered words I'd never heard about what he wanted to do to me. He said he would make me quiver, and he did. Just not the way he meant.
>
> I sought comfort from two women I thought would understand, but they could only see the moment through their own dark-tinted lenses. My experience wasn't as bad as theirs had been,

and they brushed it off. I was alone with fear and shame.

What's a girl worth?

I was 15– Too young and too scared, desperate to keep my older boyfriend, reluctantly willing. He gave me a magazine as a guide, full of bodies and skin, excitement and impossibility. He wanted me to learn what to do for him. So I did. And when he used me all up, he left me to guilt and self-loathing. And I dared not seek comfort where it had not met me before.

What's a girl worth?

I was 17– Feeling like a woman behind the wheel of my red convertible, waiting for the light to let me get to my hostess job, mature, nearly grown. He honked his horn and filled the space between his car and mine with shouts and dirty laughter: He liked how I ate my banana. I drove away stupid and small.

What's a girl worth?

I was 31– Creating a place of laughter and heart-baring, writing good words, typing out truth. I opened up so others could too and invited conversation. He was anonymous and cowardly. He sent a message to describe how he'd defile me if he had his way. I was shaken and suspicious.

When I turned to my communities, two scoffers stood out among the supporters. Women who suggested it was my fault, expected, deserved.

What's a girl worth?

I know the statement of my worth comes from the lips of the One who made me, but yet– but yet. When the shouts of men say, *You're just a thing to fuck,* when the sneers of women say, *Oh well*– the voice of truth is hard to make out through the din.

And I need the strong voices of my brothers and the sweet singing of my sisters to raise loud the truth of our Father's words, to remind me what a girl's worth.

Have you ever struggled to believe what you're
worth when God and the world disagree?

I clicked "publish" and stared at my own story on the screen, now
in full view. I was bare and frightened, bold and free. Right away,
responses flooded in, but the one that was clearest was this: I was
not alone. The question of worth was universal, and people were
aching to find it answered.

So I began to gather their stories, and I read over and over that,
different as they seemed, our stories were the same. We were all
wounded and wanting, longing for acceptance, most of all from
ourselves. And as I handled each woman's story closely and with
care, I saw my own wounds I had ignored for so long; I saw that I
needed the same close care.

And so I offer this book not as a reflection of an editor who is
herself a neatly tied-up work, but as a person who is still very
much a work in progress. I offer you stories of hurt and of healing
so that you might begin to listen to and claim your own. I offer
you hope that the story of redemption is one able to be woven into
all others. I offer you invitation to discover alongside me what a
woman is worth.

Part 1: Am I Loved?

Stories of Relationship

Introduction

Tamára Lunardo

The Man Who Mattered Most

We sing,
"How deep
The Father's love for us,
How vast
Beyond all measure,"

And I cannot
Get my mind around it;
I have
No frame of reference.

My little-girl feet
Never danced
Atop daddy-toes.

His words,
Few and harsh,
Never said,
"You are loved,
You are special,
So smart
And so funny,
Mine."

And their absence
Spoke volumes
About the worthiness
Of me.

Now I look
With gratefulness
At my own
Little girls,
And I know
That they know
Beyond a doubt
They are Daddy's.

But the ugly part of me
Looks on, jealous,
Knowing
That a lifetime of turning
To all the wrong men
Can never supplant
What was missing

From the one man
Who mattered
Most.

***

My birthfather abandoned me when I was four months old. I hadn't even had a chance to mess up, to do wrong, to earn disapproval, and yet the message was bold and clear: I was worth leaving.

My mom would do her best to tell the story over and over in love: he was abusive, and it was for my good; he loved me enough to recognize he had to let me go. I believed her as much as I could, and this was only possible because I so well believed her love of me. But in the deepest parts of my child heart, the story that I believed the most was that I was not worth holding on to. And I believed a girl who was worth giving up was not worth very much.

When I was three, my mom met a wonderful man. He bought me a Smurf drum for Christmas, which I beat with happy rhythm until it had to be held together with clear packing tape; he let me flip his necktie back over his shoulder and rewarded me with an abundantly shocked expression; he promised he would be my new daddy. But when they married just after my fourth birthday and the adoption papers were signed, our new beginning was a shock.

My dad had only ever known a father to be stern and harsh, and he became what he knew. There would be no more merriment, no more games, no "daddy." When I asked him to play Cabbage Patch dolls with me, the fun man I had known was suddenly cold and dismissive—he didn't play dolls. When I did wrong, his hand stung and his expression glowered—the hate from his eyes burned me most. I was his daughter on paper, but in real life, I was a nuisance, a troublemaker, and most certainly not his. I was betrayed by the man in whom I'd put my hope and trust, and if he could not, would not, love me like I'd thought he would, then I thought I was clearly not loveable. And I believed that an unlovable girl was worth very little.

Just before I turned six, my little brother arrived, and I was overjoyed. It was love at first sight for me and that baby boy. And it was clear that he stole our dad's heart too. But even as he grew, I could tell there was something different about the way our dad felt about him—he wasn't hard on my brother, but he was fiercely strict with me; they were close, while we were miles apart; my brother could only delight him, and I could only incur his displeasure. I could plainly, painfully see that my brother was the favorite child, and I thought it was because of something lacking in me. And I believed that a defective girl was worth less than her brother.

I have always been an emotionally demonstrative, affectionate person, and this was well met and fostered by my mom and much of my extended family. My Grandpa let me stay up past bedtime to hear his war stories, vivid and thrilling. His large, warm hands drew scenes on the kitchen table, drawing me in. My Grammie told me funny family anecdotes, and I never minded when she retold them for the tenth or twentieth time because she told them with such delight that I could not help but be delighted anew, and I was connected and reconnected to the people of these tales, to family. My mom packed short, sweet notes into my lunchbox and shared her heart in long, handwritten letters; she tucked me in to bed every night with a song and a kiss and a prayer; she massaged my shoulders when I was stressed and stroked my hair when I was tired; she held me when I cried. And I knew, because they showed me in ways I understood, that I was loved.

But my dad did not hug, did not kiss. He did not write love notes or speak encouragement. I needed to give affection, and I needed to receive it; he pushed away and withheld. I was a child longing to hear stories and to create my own, but the story I learned from my dad was that I was not wanted. And I believed that an unwanted girl was worthless.

Our relationships with people tell us a story of who we are and what we are worth. But what we believe about ourselves, and our worth, is also an author in that story. These two authors are intertwined, one always affecting the other's work. This connection is clear in each of the stories in this section. Here, women show how relationships within their family of origin, with church family, and with romantic partners have told them stories about their worth—and how their own beliefs about those stories have ultimately determined their views of themselves.

Pilar shares the pain of her mother's repeated rejections of her, and, with new love to embrace her, she lets it go. Chrystal shows how her father's demeaning treatment of her mother so insidiously and profoundly shaped her views of herself as a woman. Alise offers up a lifetime of being "other" and a message of, at last, belonging. Merritt bares the pain of trading soul for body, and she shares the beauty of a soul restored. Renee reveals the cycle of not feeling worthy of love, not receiving it, and around again, and she reveals a love that is powerful enough to break that cycle. Jennifer wrestles to answer the question of a woman's worth and finds that her family has been showing it to her all along.

Each woman's story is very much her own, but one thing is common to them all: our relationships are powerful influencers in the writing of our stories, but we can choose to guide our own beliefs. When we recognize the quiet power of our own authorship and exercise it well, we find that not only are we the more influential author, but we have the power to write a beautiful story.

The Wedding Bouquet

Pilar Elvira Wolfsteller

It is night in Patagonia, here on the banks of the mighty Rio Negro. I grip the ribbon-wrapped stems of my bouquet as tightly as I did on my wedding day a few months earlier, yearning for the same joy to return and seep through my fingers and deep into my soul. Laughter echoes through the dark from a nearby pub as I touch each of the eight pearl pins that hold the braided ivory satin in place. A chill cuts through my fleece as I study my dozen dried roses one last time. Each delicate flower is a natural work of art in faded, pastel tones, recalling a still life painting by an old Dutch master.

The simple bouquet of orange roses began its epic journey on a warm October afternoon in Virginia. On my wedding day, surrounded by the people I love, I felt complete, whole, one with my past and my present. My many lives had converged on this place; some friends had traveled halfway around the world to be with me on the day I ended what seemed like a lonesome, aimless journey across 38 years. My new husband, René, and I were no longer young, and we'd each spent too many nomadic years wandering alone. One nomad finally found the other on an Easter morning not too long before — waiting in the sun, at the end of a long and winding road.

We celebrated our wedding under a brilliant Indian summer sky to life-affirming gospel music, throwing care to the wind and love to the heavens. It was a day for raw emotion, from drunken euphoria to agonizing pain and everything in between. My mother cried bitter tears for a daughter whom she had lost to cancer years before. My brother cried for our father, also only present in spirit on a day he couldn't live to see. Cancer had taken him, too, along with his brother, our uncle, a year before.

With my head in the clouds, my simple bouquet grounded me, its existence in my hands proving my vows, my friends, my life were real. I cried for us all.

A traditional bouquet toss was out of the question from the start—all of my girlfriends were either long and happily married or long and happily divorced. Instead, I resolved to give my flowers to my mother: a gesture, like a peace offering, that I had hoped might temporarily ease some of the strain in our relationship. Disappointed in marriage and in life, still paralyzed by the tragedy of her firstborn's death almost 13 years before, she had lost the ability to express to her two adult children left living the love and devotion she showered on the one departed.

Her relationship to our older sister, in life, had not been easy. My sister was an artist, a free spirit, living an untamed life and walking in a world that our parents did not accept because they could not understand it. Her cancer crept up on me without warning, the three of them shielding me from the truth for months, and in the end left me no time to say goodbye.

After my sister died, our mother turned her into an angel who could do no wrong. Forgotten were the sharp words of criticism and ridicule, the fights and the coercion, and all those years she had locked her oldest daughter out of her life because the daughter refused to be dominated. In her new truth, my brother and I were the living, the flawed, while our sister was the virtuous, the unspoiled—the most perfect of the three siblings. Our mother could not control us two in life like she could control the memory of the adult child she lost. And that was our biggest crime.

She transformed her home into a shrine, photographs and trinkets visible from every angle. I moved on because I had to. But for our mother, time stopped. Recovery and healing she equated with forgetting, so she did not. She claimed a monopoly on mourning as if it were only her own pain that really mattered. My grief was not real or worthy to her because I did not spend my days, weeks, and years like she did, sobbing in a dark and empty room. Therefore, she concluded, I did not care enough. And she told me so. After all, I had lost "only" my sister, and not a child. My only sister.

Over the years a blinding rage toward her estranged husband—our father—had slipped into habit as she spent long afternoons at her empty kitchen table, crudely dissecting his face from family photographs with a box cutter. She banished his existence from her reality and, in so doing, tore a nearly 40-year swath of fiber from our family history.

For the past decade, an iceberg of tension floats between her and me, with a tiny tip peeking out of the water at all times. The dangerous bulk lurks below the surface, invisible to the uninitiated and deadly to the unknowing.

I did not understand the unspeakable rage she aimed at the man who housed, clothed, and fed his family of five for almost four decades and who gave us so much. That rage tore our family apart. To be fair, our father was no saint, but in her fury at his mere existence in her life, I felt more and more like an accident that she regretted having. For this reason, I have chosen to remain childless.

After the wedding ceremony she did not congratulate us, or tell us how beautiful it was, or wish us the very best for our new lives together, like the other guests did. The first thing my mother said to me was, "I couldn't stop thinking about her." The earth shifted for a moment under my feet, and I felt like the wrong daughter, standing there in white, holding my twelve orange roses, in a scene intended for someone else.

But I had made my decision about my wedding bouquet weeks earlier, and I was not about to change it now. I hoped my joy had longer legs and could outrun her sadness. And for a short, very public moment on my wedding day, I thought we could overcome what stood between us. I saw sincere appreciation in her eyes. She accepted my flowers with dignity, grace, and a smile. I hoped the moment would last.

A few days later she wrapped the bouquet in tissue paper and cautiously transported them to her home in Europe. I was touched at the care she gave them and so wanted to believe that perhaps something really had changed. The flowers occupied a place of honor on her mantelpiece for a while, the silky ivory ribbon glowing as the sun bleached color from their petals.

But the privilege didn't last. One day in January, I came home from work to find a plain brown box on my doorstep, just as the evening's blue hour encroached upon another overcast winter day. I recognized the large, angry script on the surface as my mother's; it mirrored the incensed words we had traded a few days earlier on the phone. It was the last thing I expected at the time, but later it made sense to me. She simply had never learned how to forgive.

The package sat unopened on the dining room table for nearly a week. Somehow, I instinctively knew it contained a toxin that, when released into the atmosphere, would numb me. The enclosed note read ten words, scrawled in those same careless letters on a scrap of paper torn from an old magazine: "I don't want these anymore. They give me bad vibes."

I freed my discarded bouquet from its cardboard prison and cried again. This time, René cried with me.

So here I stand, on the banks of a foreign river in the heart of Argentina, a foreign land so far from the place I call home. My father knew this country well — it is the place he was born and grew up, the place he left behind many years before to build himself a better life, and the place he longed for me to discover. The sounds of a city are somewhere distant and irrelevant. Right now I am tired, sad, and searching for some happy ending. The pain of his absence that comes and goes with the seasons is, again, here and now, so very maddeningly real.

He had asked us to bury him at sea, so all I have left to hang on to are photographs and memories and moments like this. He lives on only in my soul. I speak to him in whispers and I take him with me on all of my adventures. He sees me and guides me, even today, even now.

My mother still lives, but her maternal love, it seems, is no longer unconditional. To this day, not a single wedding photo of mine hangs on the walls of her home; she ignores my husband and is blind to my happiness. Simple emotional neglect has turned into active hostility as the Christmas gifts I send are returned to me unwrapped and my attempts at civilized communication are left unanswered. She has elected to lock me out of her life as she did to my sister many years before — history repeating itself. Perhaps if I got sick and died, my status would change. But I will never know.

Methodically I remove the pearl pins one by one and unwind the satin ribbon. It is my souvenir to keep, to forever remind me of a husband's love found and a mother's love lost; of what remains and also of what is gone. I trust the Rio Negro's swift black current will carry my bouquet to my father—wherever he is, everywhere and nowhere, just beyond the horizon, in a place I cannot see. Under the light of the Southern Cross, and with René at my side, I send my flowers on their final journey.

Lesson Learned: The Handicap of Being Born Female

Chrystal Westbrook Southwell

I don't remember how old I was when I first knew my mother was not very smart. I knew this, of course, because my father told me so. He never looked me in the eyes and said, "Your mother isn't very smart." Instead, in both small and large ways, he belittled her intelligence, her emotions, and her commitment to family. I learned what a woman is worth by watching how my father treated my mother.

Mom grew up the dearly loved, only daughter in a family full of boys. Her dad farmed and her mom worked a full-time job in town to bring in steady income. As a result, at the age of nine she became responsible for taking care of her younger brothers and much of the housework. As a teenager, she prayed and asked God to allow her to marry a minister. In her small farming town, the minister was one of the most educated and admired members of the community.

Mom played piano from the time she was a small girl. She was an accomplished musician and had been the pianist for the church she grew up in as well as for every church Dad ever pastored. She also played and sang as part of a women's trio for several years. She played almost entirely by ear but was also able to read simple chord charts. Her face always lit up when she had an opportunity to play.

Our family frequently sang "specials" together in church, with Mom accompanying on the piano, Dad on the guitar, and all of us singing. Preparation for these invariably entailed several lengthy practice sessions. Dad usually picked out the music we would sing. Each song had to meet his requirement of not sounding "too country," a musical style he despised; unfortunately, he married a woman who was primarily a country musician.

Dad dropped the needle onto the record to play a new song. Mom began to pick out the song and play along with the record. Almost immediately Dad found something wrong with the way she was playing the music. "No, no — that's not the right harmony. You're missing it!" Mom would try again. Again, the harmony wasn't what he wanted, or the rhythm didn't replicate the recording, or something wasn't exactly what he had in mind. Then the frustrated grimaces began. "Ergh... I wish I could just play it myself. You're the pianist — can't you hear that rhythm?!" My sister and I stood quietly, willing the practice time to finish quickly.

Mom rarely, if ever, defended herself and never raised her voice. She loved music and playing the piano. Yet her joy in playing was wounded a little at a time. Her belief in her ability to play was chipped away. Even now, years later, she believes she has no sense of rhythm. I learned that a woman's abilities are never good enough.

I was ten and sitting in the family room in the basement. There was a *bump, bump* noise coming down the stairs — my parents were moving the recliner chair. I heard a grunt and then, "What are you doing?!" Mom's answer was difficult to hear. "I thought we were....." His voice cut her off. "Don't think — just do what I tell you!" I learned that a woman's thoughts aren't worth hearing.

Dad would frequently work from his office at home. As he sat at his typewriter, writing out sermon notes or an article, he would call out to Mom, requesting the spelling of a word. Regardless of what Mom was doing, he expected her to respond immediately with the correct spelling since "she'd been a good speller in school." Dad owned a large, unabridged dictionary that sat on a shelf in his office. However, he said it was distracting to stop and look up how to spell a word when he was in the middle of getting his thoughts captured on paper. Rather than expressing frustration with the frequent interruptions to her own work, Mom patiently answered every spelling request. I learned that a woman's work is less important than a man's.

Typically, Sundays were incredibly full days, with services in the morning and evening plus Sunday School. There was never time to eat dinner before the Sunday night service, so we ate a light meal after the service. These meals were usually sandwiches or scrambled eggs. But I looked forward to those special occasions when we were hosting a guest minister or when one of the parishioners invited us out for an after-service meal, as this frequently meant we would have pizza.

One Sunday night as we got into the car after a long day of services, Dad looked expectantly at Mom and said, "Why don't we have *p-i-z-z-a* tonight?" She looked at him quizzically, not picking up that he was spelling out the word. He repeated, "I said, why don't we have *p-i-z-z-a*?!" His frustration at her lack of understanding was evident in his tone and facial expression. Finally I couldn't stand the tension any more. "Mom," I burst out, "Dad's saying he wants to have pizza tonight!"

The light of understanding hit my mom's face, and she agreed that pizza was a great idea. Dad asked Mom how she could possibly not have understood what he was saying when even the *children* understood it. Mom's response to being made fun of was to smile and try to join in the appreciation of the "joke." I learned that women are slow-witted and, while they can't help being slow, it's still appropriate to make them objects of ridicule. As a young child, I learned how to join my dad in belittling my mom.

Every year we drove cross-country from wherever Dad was pastoring at the time to visit Mom's family. The trip was at least two 16-hour days of driving with few stops and many tense comments from Dad about how much he hated the trip and visiting Mom's family. At the end of these visits, there was always a tearful goodbye scene between Mom and her parents. As we drove away from my grandparents' home, while Mom was still wiping away her tears, Dad told her, again, how foolishly emotional she and her parents were to cry when saying goodbye. He said it showed she had an unhealthy relationship with her parents that kept her from putting *him* first. I learned that a woman is foolish and immature if she wants to maintain a close relationship with her parents and siblings.

Of course, the inevitable crisis erupted as I entered my teen years. I began to grapple with a soul-searing dilemma. A woman was slow-witted, had abilities that were never good enough, had thoughts that weren't worth hearing, had work that was less important than a man's, was foolish and immature. And yet, as some sort of impossible test, God had cruelly set me up for failure by creating me female. I wasn't going to be able to avoid becoming one of those objects of pity and ridicule. The best I could hope to do was mitigate the unfortunate circumstance of my gender. I determined to be the smartest, the quickest-witted, the toughest. I would allow no clinging relationships with family. I would think like a man and ensure my thoughts would be heard.

As part of a pastor's family, I lived a nomadic life with frequent long-distance moves. By the time I started high school, I was entering my fourteenth school. To ensure I didn't encourage clinging relationships, I decided not to maintain contact with any of my friends after we moved. In fact, I taught myself to entirely redirect my thoughts away from memories of my prior homes so that I wouldn't be tempted to dwell on previous relationships and somehow be identified as a woman who needed to cling to others.

I loved basketball, but I didn't believe I could play it well or, for that matter, perform well at any sport. Dad frequently remarked on Mom's lack of physical coordination, and my assumption was that I must be uncoordinated as well. So rather than risk exposing this supposed lack of ability, I opted to become the basketball team trainer and scorekeeper. This at least allowed me to participate in a small way in the sport I enjoyed so much without risk that my greatly feared inadequacies would be discovered.

To help combat any question of whether I was smart enough, I focused on ensuring my success in school. I determined that I would make the best grades, hopefully in my entire class. I frequently had one of the highest test scores and was frustrated any time that I didn't. I decided to add the input of my teachers to the case I was building internally that I was smart enough. I relished the relationships I established with my teachers who told me how smart I was. I thought surely their assessments of my abilities would count for something in my ongoing search to confirm my own worth.

Ah, but the crying—that was the hardest to manage. My life had taught me that only women, who were apparently prone to emotional immaturity, were likely to cry. Saying goodbye to family at the end of a visit, watching a bittersweet scene in a movie, weathering a disappointment—any of these experiences could threaten tears that needed to be prevented. However, the circumstance to be avoided at all costs was to cry in front of Dad. That would have proven that I was no better than Mom. I developed a method of stopping my tears that was almost foolproof. Any time I felt the tears pricking behind my eyelids, I would bite down hard on the inside of my cheeks. Focusing on the pain in my mouth invariably gave me the ability to shut off the tears.

Whether it was ruthlessly severing relationships, or avoiding experiences that might expose my inadequacies, or panting after the approval of my teachers, or drawing blood as I bit my cheeks to keep from crying, or a long list of other choices I made, I got it. I understood. My worth would be proved by how well I overcame the handicap of being born female.

The Distance Between

Alise D. Wright

The distance between being quirky and lonely can feel miniscule.

I was the girl who was everybody's friend. I was funny and nice and smart and loud and weird. I played the alto sax in band, the piano in chorus, and the bad girl in school musicals.

In real life, I was always the good girl. I don't know if I'd ever heard the "I don't drink or smoke or chew and I don't go with boys who do" rhyme while I was in high school, but I'm sure most would have assumed that it applied to me. I was virginal and chaste. I'd like to say this was because of my strong moral fiber, but mostly it was because there weren't any inquiries. It was easy to maintain my virginity when no one was interested in procuring it. It was easy to look virtuous when no one wanted to tarnish my virtue.

Most of the time, I could convince myself that it didn't matter. I embraced my weirdness. I would call myself "band geek" before anyone else could. I wore black clothes and strange makeup and cut my hair differently — things that would ensure that I would still have friends but that any lack of interest in me wasn't because I wasn't pretty or desirable, but because I was just too out there for our small-town high school boys to handle.

The distance between unique and ugly can feel tiny.

I never wanted to be reduced to my looks, but honestly, once or twice it would have been nice to be the one being asked to the dance. To be the one who had plans with a boy on a Saturday night. To be the one who turned heads.

Instead, I joked with the boy I liked at the cast party and then went home and cried for hours because he confided that he wanted to date my friend, not me. I exposed my heart to another potential boyfriend only to be told that he just wanted to be friends; he didn't feel "that way" about me. Time after time I was passed over, ignored, sidelined. These relationships were just for the normal girls, not for me.

I wasn't exactly rejected — I just wasn't pursued.

The distance between a 16-year-old girl and a 30-year-old woman can feel puny.

I was sitting in a living room with two people who had told me that they loved me. They had told me that they supported me. They had told me that they wanted me to be a part of what they were doing. I had explained to them just what I wanted to do with the music at their church — at *our* church — and they had agreed that I was capable of implementing my plan and that the ideas that I was presenting were beneficial to the church body.

Eventually I began implementing these changes: more solo voices, longer instrumental breaks, newer songs. I had run these things by the pastors; they weren't surprises for those in leadership. But they were surprises for the congregation, and those surprises were upsetting for some. I received a letter outlining how the changes were distracting and not God-honoring. There were meetings scheduled with the pastor to which I was invited. There were meetings to which I was not invited. And in the midst of all of these letters and meetings, the people who had told me that they loved and supported me reneged on all of their promises. The love turned into frustration; the support turned into reprimands. And I was no longer welcome.

Oh, they didn't say that. They didn't kick me out of the church. They still said that they loved me and supported me. It was just that they believed that I was no longer submissive enough. I was no longer embracing the vision of the church. I was just a little too different, too loud, too weird. I could attend church there, but I couldn't attend as a musician, doing the one thing that I was created to do. That was for the normal people who conformed to the way things always were, not for me.

I wasn't exactly rejected — I just wasn't pursued.

The distance between being abused and being rejected can feel microscopic.

We're aware of the ways that women are harmed by abuse, and it is horrific. In no way do I mean to diminish the pain that happens when women are hurt directly by violent actions and by harsh words or when women are rejected strictly because of their sex rather than being judged on the merit of their work. My heart breaks when I think of the ways that girls and women are violated every day by men, other women, and by the Church.

But there is also pain in not being pursued. For a long time I ignored that pain because it seemed selfish or shallow to be upset about not having a date to the prom or being told that I couldn't play the piano in a church. They were such seemingly small offenses that it was difficult to admit how deeply they affected me beyond the initial occurrence. It seemed easier to simply pretend that I wasn't bothered by them.

But denying these emotions did not spare me from the consequences. I experienced deep depressions, difficulties with my weight, and a diminished sense of self. I tied my worth to the rejection I experienced for being the woman that God created me to be rather than finding it in the Creator himself.

I now know that these stories are not the full measure of me. I have been pursued — by an unfailing God; by a faithful husband; by people who refuse to allow me to be counted strictly by what I can provide for them, but, rather, give me permission to be wholly myself. I cling to these relationships because they allow me to see that my value is far greater than what I can see on my own. They help me know that I am loved, and they encourage me to love myself.

The distance between where I was and where I am is enormous.

Being Set Free

Merritt Onsa

Six or seven, maybe eight—though it hardly matters that I don't remember my age—I was too young to understand the verbal accosting of a boy in the neighborhood park. "I wanna see your cabbage," he taunted. I had no idea what he was talking about, but something told me he wasn't safe.

In sixth grade, I was fake-married to an older boy as part of a game my friends played at school. The pretend relationship became real, and I was "going with" a seventh grader. Our secret make-out sessions in somewhat public places were an inner battle in my mind between "yes" and "no." *I don't want him to touch me there; only bad girls would do that… so why does it feel so good?* I was too timid to acknowledge—much less speak—what I wanted or thought was right.

By 13, my heart and flesh ached to possess the kind of love I'd seen on TV and in movies. And then another boy entered in to supply it. I was a hardly-developed girl in a bathing suit playing with friends at dusk in the final days of summer. He was a 16-year-old boy in a big truck, headlights blaring in my eyes. I was vulnerable, watched, admired, desired—the powerful attention of an older boy melted me, and he quickly became my world.

I barely had the maturity to choose or be chosen by a boyfriend, but my mother's attempts to remind me I was too young did nothing to persuade me of my naiveté about relationships. Convinced that, in him, I now possessed everything I'd ever dreamed of, I dove headfirst into a clandestine teenage love affair. We spent every possible waking moment together and lied to avoid discovery and our parents' disapproval.

I believed every confession of love he uttered to me—even when friends warned me about him. *They don't know what they're talking about. He truly loves me.* He promised we'd be together forever even if we were forced apart and had to meet again later in life. We made a secret pact.

When I told him I wasn't ready for sex, he said it was okay. And then he denied rumors that he was getting his needs met someplace else. Of course, I believed him. And I was convinced enough to do everything else he desired sexually.

My parents' rejection of our "love" gave me justification for sneaking around. I *had* to be with him. And I became an expert at hiding in closets, crawling out bedroom windows, racing the clock to beat my mom home from work at the end of the day, plotting secret phone calls while grounded, and orchestrating late-night rendezvous.

We were finally discovered the night I lost my virginity. I was 14. Our deception and lies were overthrown by the truth my parents uncovered in the backseat of their car. Escape was futile, yet silence was the only defense I could conjure as shame opened up and swallowed me whole. And he, who had professed his love and devotion to me, betrayed his allegiance and told my parents I was to blame.

I was grounded, and he was off limits. He wasn't allowed in our house, and I wasn't allowed to go out. But still we found a way. When it seemed we'd reached the limit of forbidden behavior, the flood gates opened wide. His job at a video store gave us easy late-night access to pornography, and he taught me what it meant to *really* love a man.

The following year, when he sought my permission to invite the prettiest girl in school to the senior prom, I finally understood who I was to him: nothing.

But at least now I knew.

Now the foundation was set; I was learned in the ways of men— what they wanted from me and how easily I captured their attention. High school boys were still interesting, but working at a local grocery store, I attracted the attention of men far beyond my age. Such power was captivating.

And somehow I believed attraction would guarantee what I really wanted: love and a lasting relationship. But time after time, physical relationships I thought were based on love came up dry, and I was left in a ball of tears—empty, hurt, and alone.

In college, I wanted a change, but it didn't take long to fall into a similar pattern of seeking approval from men and attempting to secure their love through a physical relationship. I would meet a guy, become obsessed with him, and get involved physically— *that's what you do in college, right?* And I'd hope with all hope that this one would be "the one." He never was.

My insecurities ran wild and controlled my every thought, deed, and overindulgence in alcohol. I was never enough for him. Or I was too much. So, when relationships weren't working, weekend college parties provided plenty of options for hooking up. Some of those efforts "succeeded" in the short term: *At least he couldn't reject me if we both knew it was just one night.* Although I tried to be unfazed, "accomplishing" a one-night stand with the guy I'd chosen for the night did nothing but make me feel worse. If there could be anything emptier than emptiness, it was the deep, dark hole growing in my heart.

It wasn't until a friend forced himself on me after a party one night that I began to connect my promiscuity with the constant heartbreak I felt. When one of my roommates mocked my tears and suggested I'd had it coming, I was overwhelmed with grief, shame, and fear. *What if she was right?*

After college, determined to soothe the hurt of my past with the hope for true love, I spent the next decade "shopping" for a husband. One kind man I dated in graduate school was Jewish. When I wasn't willing to convert, he moved out of state. Several others were eager for a physical relationship but weren't ready to commit—at least not to me.

At 28, I thought I'd finally met the one. He wooed and romanced me, and I took it in stride when he solidified the break-up with his ex on the night of our first date. A year later we moved in together, but shortly after, everything began to fall apart. My disinterest, his pornography habit, our inability to communicate—it was a recipe for disaster.

I eventually cheated on him and our tumultuous break-up ultimately led us both to Jesus. And though I was comforted by the grace and healing promised in my newfound faith, my wounds were alive and well, even if they were buried under layers of self-protection.

When it seemed I couldn't go a day without crying, a friend recommended Celebrate Recovery, the 12-step program at our church. Soon I began to uncover my self-loathing and forgive the boys and men who'd knowingly and unknowingly helped me trash my self-worth. All the while, wise and encouraging women spoke words of healing into my heart about my inherent worth, and they told me how precious I was to God.

They also shared an idea that seemed absurd to me—that I could save myself sexually for my future husband. I wanted it to be true for me, but *was it possible?* A rule-follower at heart, I believed maybe I could white-knuckle this thing until my true Prince Charming came along. Maybe, with just some minor faltering. I didn't get it, but as I eventually began to connect my pain and lack of self-worth to my past promiscuity, I chose to believe these women knew something that I couldn't, at this point, understand.

So when a conference called Intimate Issues came to town, I decided to go—alone. I knew I needed to be there just for me. Not with friends. Not for social hour. Just for me.

About halfway through the first morning, one of the speakers pressed pause in the agenda. Before she would go any further in the curriculum, she wanted to be sure we had all dealt with the hurt in our lives related to our past sexual experiences. She began to share her interpretation of a Bible story from Luke, Chapter 7, in which an "immoral woman" anoints Jesus.

> *In the story, we aren't told if she lost her virginity by force or because she had chosen to give it away. Either way, it meant she had no value as a bride, so she may have turned to prostitution as a means to support herself.*
>
> *As you might imagine, everyone in town knew of her shameful lifestyle. Children mocked her and threw rocks at her. Appropriate women crossed to the other side of*

the street so as not to walk near her. She was ashamed, and she longed to be free.

When she heard Jesus was in town, she remembered that He was known to spend time with sinners, and she knew He healed people. She discovered where He was one night, and she went to the Pharisee's home with an expensive jar of perfume.

When she came into the presence of His holiness, she understood the depth of her sin and hung her head in shame. She immediately knelt at His feet and began to weep. If you can picture the pain and shame in her life, you might imagine that each tear she cried at His feet was a confession for each man she had been with.

When she lifted her head and realized the mess she had made, she wiped her tears from Jesus' feet with her own hair. Peace surrounded her, and she sensed God wiping away her sin. Out of joy and thankfulness for His forgiveness, she began kissing Jesus' feet, cherishing Him and adoring Him.

Finally, she remembered the bottle of perfume she'd brought along. Maybe it was the same perfume she'd used each time another man came to her bed. Knowing that she was forgiven and would never need it again, she poured it out in its entirety on His feet.

As the speaker told this story, I so deeply identified with the immoral woman. I had been sitting there quietly when she said, "Forget your friends, ladies. Forget who you are sitting with. If you have business to do with the Lord, as this woman did, get up from your seat and go wherever you need to in this room to kneel at Jesus' feet."

I was in the middle of what felt like a very long row of seats. *There's no way I'm standing up and making all these people move for me,* I thought.

But it was not for me to decide. With tears streaming down my face, my body hurled itself over the women sitting in my row. Once in the aisle, I ran to the darkest corner I could find in the back of the room. My legs collapsed, and I fell to my knees.

Every name, every face, every incident that had solidified my feelings of worthlessness—I wept and prayed it out at His feet. I could see in my mind's eye the nail marks in Jesus' feet that were there for me. The price that was paid so that I might be free. The great worth that God said belonged to me.

An older woman approached my convulsing body; she placed her hands gently on my back and began to quietly pray for me. When the tears stopped, she held me close, looked deep into my eyes, and told me that as she was praying she felt the Holy Spirit guide her prayer. She said, "I believe God is going to use your story for good."

I know today that it was not by my own power that I finally, truly let go of the hurt from my past. For years I told myself I was strong and independent, that I didn't need to feel bad for the choices I'd made. But no matter how I rationalized it, the countless times I gave my heart and body away for nothing in return haunted me and the damage ached in my soul. But that day, I knew my worth—declared by Christ—and acknowledged by a complete stranger who loved me in the midst of my mess.

Walking away from the conference, I felt complete freedom. I knew deep in my soul that absolutely nothing could keep me from the love of Christ—not my present, not my past, not even the years I had spent running after someone or something to fill my deepest longing. Promiscuity had broken my heart and held me captive. I now know that God in heaven is the one who defines my worth, and He says I am lovely, beautiful, beloved, and adored. And believing that is what sets me free.

Winter

Renee Ronika

"When you gonna make up your mind? When you gonna love you as much as I do?" – Tori Amos

At the Phoenician Resort in May, a woman wearing a white dress with no bra walked past my husband Greg and me as we began a meal that I wasn't sure wouldn't be the last of our life together. We both tried not to look as her breasts held themselves high underneath filmy fabric.

Mine were ample from nursing our ten-month-old daughter Ariel, and that evening I was adorned in stilettos and enough cleavage, I had hoped, to hold my husband's attention. Later, Greg left to use the restroom at the same time as the woman in white. I watched them walk away. I gasped, sipped Merlot, and asked aloud, "Lord, what am I going to do?"

When I turned back around and faced my husband's vacated seat, I saw Jesus. He looked at me and said, "Renee, it's going to be okay."

Flurrying through my mind were the text messages from another woman that I had found two weeks earlier on Greg's phone. They were frozen in my memory.

Eight months before this, in November, when my husband had returned home from his doctoral music classes and spun the globe to find this woman's hometown, I asked what he was looking for. "There's a new student in the program. She's from here."

I looked at Greg; the wild abandon in his eyes betrayed him. "Do you have a crush on her?"

"No, Renee."

Greg was not a liar, but I knew the look he hadn't realized he wore, the one that said he was more curious than he let on. "You have a crush on her!" I laughed.

"Renee, I love you."

I didn't think about her again. I had no reason to: Greg was a man known by his faithfulness, his maturity, his ability to commit. His cheating on me hadn't entered my mind.

Even still, plaguing me throughout our three-year marriage had been the memory of our wedding, on an unusually frigid December day in Phoenix, when one of my bridesmaids announced to 140 reception attendees the question I had asked her the night Greg and I got engaged: Was Greg too good looking for me? Our guests laughed along with her at the question's absurdity. I sat bewildered by her divulgence and swallowed back sobs. Now everyone in the room would wonder — if they hadn't already — why someone like my husband would choose someone like me.

I had believed in the myth of marriage: being loved would heal the wounds of violence and rejection. Instead of dealing with my history of abuse — by men from childhood and church members from adulthood — I lived in sanctified denial. I sabotaged myself when I pretended to live a new life without recognizing any ramifications of abuse.

Greg married me because he cherished me as vibrant, intelligent, articulate, attractive. After we got married and moved to Colorado for his graduate studies, however, I retreated into silence — forsaking conversation, writing, and ministry. I evaded Greg emotionally, yet freely and frequently offered him sex, the part of marriage I focused on entirely.

Vulnerability was troubling to negotiate. I didn't feel confident enough in Greg's love for me to reveal my true heart to him. I also had been having violent dreams of my past — the molesters, the alcoholics, the vituperators — and Greg wanted to know why I wouldn't open up to him about it. It was a cold February night, a few months before I found the messages, and Greg and I were in bed, my head nestled between his arm and chest. "Because if you knew all the ugly that's in my past," I whispered, "I'm afraid you would reject me like everyone else has."

Greg held me tighter. "Renee, I want to know all of it so I can rescue you from it."

I began to weep. I recalled a time during our engagement when I still wasn't sure why Greg was marrying me. I had gotten imposingly ill, and Greg laid his hand on my head, gazing into my eyes with a love I knew was not concocted. That same trust entered me now.

But the nightmares continued. I awoke during some with a demon next to my bed, looking into my eyes, taunting me. I screamed, hid under the blanket, and allowed Greg to hold and pray over me as I trembled.

By April, nothing had improved. Although I wanted to change, I didn't know how to allow myself to love and be loved. I finally went before my God, the One who had rescued me so often before, and said, "Lord, whatever it takes, heal me."

The following week, I gathered up courage to show Greg my true feelings for him, to participate in my marriage as an invited guest instead of an interloper. I planned a just-between-us celebration to honor an academic milestone. I felt proud to be the first one to express my exuberance to him. That was the day I found the text messages. He had already celebrated his victory with her.

She was like the women from his past—women who looked and behaved the opposite of me. Where they had blue, I had brown; where they were flirtatious, I was withdrawn. But where they were coy, I was direct.

That evening, I searched for divorce papers online to absolve Greg of any moral obligation to stay with me. The affair at this point had only been emotional, so I told him to go have sex with her. "I don't fight for men, Greg. If you want her and not me, I'm gone."

For years I had scampered off to different states to start anew, to see if the life I wanted—the one I believed I deserved—would be waiting for me. But in every location the outcome resulted in my departure—alone—headed toward grass that was never green enough. I hadn't expected to be doing this again in my marriage, but here I was, confronted with the same reflexive instinct.

After filling out the divorce papers, I left my laptop open—the white light from the monitor glaring—to attend to Ariel's dinner. She sat in her highchair, screaming uncontrollably. I attempted to pacify her until an alarm sounded from within. I rushed back to my computer and closed the Internet window, the laptop lid. When I returned to the dining table, peace overcame Ariel. I closed my eyes and exhaled; to my cynical mind, her reaction indicated I would have to stay in a marriage with a man who wanted to be with someone else. In my spirit, however, I knew this meant my marriage would be healed.

The next morning, late April, after weeks of 70-degree weather, we woke to accumulating snow, the sudden return of winter. Before the sun stretched into the sky, the snow was gone, as if it had never been there at all.

Greg announced that he chose me, deciding to honor his vow instead of his infatuation. The spiritual man within him foresaw a holy destiny with me versus a hedonistic rampage with her. But I could see him holding on; I perceived when his thoughts drifted toward her. We were standing on ice that was ready to give, to split far enough apart to take us each away unchanged.

Once the semester was over in May, we escaped the too-familiar as a family to Phoenix, my hometown, driving through the Rockies to descend upon the desert, where we hoped to find oasis. Pornographic billboards tried seducing us into casinos. We kept our eyes on the road, praying out the oppression of the wasteland, the lust.

On our first morning in Phoenix we welcomed its arid spring air. It felt like summer. But as I lay in bed, cold enveloped me. I felt my will to live escaping. Only the thought of Ariel drew me back. It would be months until I fought off death entirely, until I overcame the lie that my departure would allow for Greg's freedom.

Greg purposed to show his love for me and ushered me away to the Phoenician Resort. I accompanied him in black, and as we sat across from each other, I searched his every facial tic and slide of finger around the wine glass to discern if I could still see her. I wanted my husband back, but I needed Jesus to remind me of why

I was here, of how I had entered into a marriage that confirmed my misgivings: my husband saw me as I saw myself—entirely replaceable.

After dinner that night, we drove my father's cherry red Mercedes convertible to the base of South Mountain and sat with the top down under a shroud of stars. My strength astonished me. Forgiveness overwhelmed me. A supernatural force, one I was familiar with, permeated me and, in my mind's eye, I saw Greg in a classroom. In the vision, a bright light appeared over the woman, who was sitting next to him.

"Greg," I looked at him in the passenger seat. His shoulders were slumped. "Did something happen when you were in a classroom with her?"

Greg thought for a moment. "That's when it first happened. I glanced at her and felt lightning. It was as if she and I were meant to be together."

"It was demonic, Greg. It's all a lie. She's a deception." I swallowed back tears. "I'm your wife."

Greg looked up at the mountains. "I know. It never felt right with her." He looked at me. "But that confidence is what was missing for so long in our relationship."

I met Greg's gaze. "I'm your wife."

We prayed there in the desert, moonlight illuminating the shadowy places. I felt deception lift from Greg. He told me he loved me, and I knew then that his love not only reached back but even farther forward, and it would grow. For the first time in our marriage I told Greg without reservation that I loved him. There, in the front seat of the convertible, Greg and I repeated our marriage vows to each other. That night we conceived our daughter Eva.

In the time spanning the fertile valleys of Arizona and the pregnant peaks of Colorado, Greg and I have discovered a love deep for each other. We look at each other differently, the solemnity of our vows present in our eyes. For our fourth wedding anniversary, the completion of our year of grief, Greg declared his love for me by writing a song cycle based on the Song of Songs. As he sang these words over me, he wept while I felt the rush of the Holy Spirit making everything new:

Arise, my love, make haste, my dove,

my beautiful one, and come.

For winter is now past;

the rain is over and gone. (vv. 2:10-11)

Before I found out about my husband's indiscretion, I had prayed out fear and insecurity, knowing the process might hurt. My perceived rejection by Greg would seem an ironical answer to a genuine prayer, but God did not cause the emotional infidelity in my marriage, just as He did not intend for me to be sexually molested, verbally assailed, or emotionally abused. These experiences simply contributed to my attitude of defeat.

I am now in possession of a holy secret: the Enemy speaks the opposite of what the Lord declares over me. Satan bombards me with messages of failure; he reminds me that I am alone.

He is a liar.

I have been released from the torment of self-fulfilling curses, of believing, then discovering, that I am not worth the blessings God has predestined for me. In looking back, I see a girl who was so afraid of being loved, who even resolved that she didn't care either way if she was loved, finally realize that not only does she deserve it, but she has it. I have accepted the invitation to the banquet table, where I sit beside Jesus, where I am white as snow.

These days, Greg admires me often. When I wonder aloud about parts of me that still aspire toward better, he says, "When I look at you, Renee, I don't see any flaws."

I believe him.

On Belonging

Jennifer Luitwieler

I tried. I really did. Three fingers poised for a scout's salute. At least I think that's three fingers; I barfed at one of my first Girl Scout meetings and never returned for the shame of it. Too much soda. Anyway, I tried to keep the tone way down. I tried to answer the question of a woman's worth without getting shrill, or hand wavy, or arching my eyebrows. Talking about the value of a woman, as a gendered human, just sets my pistons firing.

I'm lucky, I guess. I learned early and daily that the value of a woman is exactly identical to the value of a man—equal. The value of all humans is equal. I might have read something about this in one of those old documents printed in blood on sheep gut. I seem to recall something like, "all men are created equal…"[1] And even farther back, "in Him there is neither slave nor free, male nor female."

I learned the worth of a woman from my parents. Growing up, our days were a flurry of activities. From sun up to sun down we launched headlong into practices, church groups, meetings, school, homework; my siblings and I were all over town. Mom rose before the sun to get ready for her commute downtown. She'd pull out of the drive as we stood at the bus stop, in the dark, in our coats, blinking into the dawn. Dad left the house soon after the bus trundled us off to school.

---

1   I will refrain here from inserting my screed regarding the scope of the word *men* in the American Constitution.

We were like timed magnets, blasting apart and thrust back together, to the bosom of the hearth, as if regrouping were essential to our breath—and perhaps it was. Despite our bickering and our tension common to all families, we liked each other. And we were busy. Like everyone else.

But Saturdays were different. Saturdays were for rest. Sundays might be rest for most people, but our dad was a pastor, and Sunday was for church, and that was rarely restful. If something like Grandparents was happening on Saturday—and if you knew my grandparents, they certainly happened—then Dad was up early, shoving the vacuum cleaner into my closed door, a not-so-gentle hint to get up and get moving. He's so smooth, my dad.

But there were Saturdays when there were no games, no practices, no events. On these days, the sound of public radio streamed from my parents' adjacent room. Dad stumbled around the kitchen, making pancakes or eggs and sausage. I heard coffee blurping in the percolator, the clang of dishes being pulled from cupboards and set on the table, Dad practicing his sermon. From my parents' room, the sound of a page turning, a sheet shifting, told me Mom was awake. This was my cue.

When I heard her waking, I'd pad across the hall into their room and crawl into bed with Mom and her book. I read the back copy of her books, waiting. My sister usually joined us, we girls flanking her as we did when we stood by her in church, happy to be still and quiet and with her. We lay motionless, just breathing, sometimes dozing. As she read, Mom took our hands and pinched the nail beds, a reassuring touch. The nail bed pinch somehow made all our very important teenage drama okay, or ever so slightly less dramatic. Eventually, laughter ebbed into the room with the rising sun, its yellowy fingers gliding through the windows, into the corners of our eyes. The too-quiet, too-calm voice of the public radio announcer made one of us giggle; his enunciations were so clear and practiced and self-important. Someone mimicked his tone or made a joke about it, and our day of talk began.

By the time our dad brought Mom her first cup of coffee, a habit he still practices today, we were awake and talking, laughing, telling stories, remembering the funny thing the choir lady did on Wednesday or the use of quotes around "pineapples" at the "grocery" store.

When Dad handed Mom her coffee, she turned her face to him in wordless thanks, his big hands offering the mug, and his heart, and a hot breakfast. Their eyes always met. I love this about my parents: They know how to look at each other. Then, he walked back to the kitchen to turn the sausage and flip the omelette.

Saturday breakfast when no one had to dash off was a leisurely perk tucked inside the mania of every week. For the women in the family, this simply meant moving our chatter from the bedroom to the kitchen. Even our brother, the eldest child, the surly teen, made an appearance at this breakfast table, allowing himself to be teased, laughing with a guileless ease he refused to match when we passed him in the hall at school. We sat in our jammies, being brought plates of hot food, pouring glass after glass of juice or milk, until someone finally made a move for the shower. The shower gesture was the benediction, the last gasp of togetherness before lurching headlong into another day of rambling about, the family magnet bursting apart for another interval, skyrocketing through our little planet.

Saturday breakfasts were an in situ lesson on what a woman is worth.

The dictionary tells us that worth means, among other things, "sufficiently good, important, or interesting to justify a specified action; deserving to be treated or regarded in the way specified." It also refers to "the value equivalent to that of someone or something under consideration." Finally, worth is "the level at which something or someone deserves to be valued or rated."[2]

I try not to talk too much about the worth of a woman because when I do, the merest hint of shrill crazy-lady appears, an apparition emanating opinion and disgust. I get irritated that the conversation is still being held nearly 100 years after women earned the right to vote. Two hundred years after a super fancy document declared that "all men are created equal," women still make seventy cents to every dollar a man makes for the same job. We argue about maternity leave, breastfeeding, and whether women should return to work. If a woman stays home, others want to mandate how she stays home. If a woman works outside the home, others try to control how she does that. We are told how to dress our age, how to give birth, how to parent. It is easy, in our culture, to get an

2   Oxford American Dictionaries.

opinion on how women should be doing everything they should be doing.

These theoretical debates only add fuel to the so-called "mommy wars" currently besieging America, and none of them actually addresses the issue: What is a woman worth? (And what does it have to do with breakfast?)

A woman, as a person with agency and intent, is a powerful entity. A woman, as a person, is of value. Plain and simple. I learned this at Saturday breakfast. Of course, breakfast was only one place the value of a woman was modeled in my home and in my life. One does not receive a valuable lesson once but is a student of that lesson for life.

In the quiet welcome my mother gave us, to simply sit with her, I knew my presence was wanted. In her eyes that seemed to hear my words as much as her ears did, I learned that my voice mattered, even when she did not understand or agree. In her quiet touch, the soft pinch of fingertip on fingertip, I learned that she desired to comfort me, to be with me, to know me. And when I asked her for advice or an opinion, her words taught me she had, in fact, sought to hear me and had chosen her words with a precision I wish I could practice, even now.

When my dad handed my mom her first cup of coffee, I saw what a man will do for a woman. He will bring her coffee in bed so that she can sit quietly alone and then sit quietly with her daughters. He will make her breakfast because she likes it. He will bring her books she will enjoy from the library, because she is on his mind, though his lips rarely whisper the love he so clearly shows.

I always understood my worth as a human, as a woman, because of my parents. I knew, because they told me, that there were no limits before me except those I didn't attempt to climb. I understood that questions worth asking were questions worth answering and that, if I wanted, I could search for those answers. Watching my mother bundle up every morning for a cold bus ride downtown, I knew women were capable of hard work. Seeing her smile in the face of a backhanded familial compliment, I learned that opening one's mouth does not always gain the desired result.

The older I get, the more I appreciate my mother and want to be like her, as a person and as a mother. She listened to me with her whole body, while I find myself murmuring, "uh huh, uh huh," as a child tells a seemingly endless story. When I begin to get shrill about the worth of a woman, she peers at me, her face as calm and unflagging as a pool, and I am at once called to surrender my angst and curious about the depths of that serenity.

When I think about the worth of a woman, I can't help but think about the woman, and the man, who gave me the clearest picture of human worth. My parents, flawed beings surely, cling to each other, cling to love because, I think, they know its power. They understand the worth of each other and because they showed it, openly and out loud, I understand: I am worth something because I am loved.

But still I struggle to define a woman's worth. In my limited experience with humanity, people are complicated and messy and sometimes idiot jerk-faces. In the first few descriptors from the definition, "sufficiently good or important," I realize that I might need to tweak my idea of good or important because sometimes it just means, "those people I like who don't irritate me."

I ascribe to the idea that men and women were created in the image of a loving and holy God. This means I must recognize God as the arbiter of worth, whether we are perfect or imperfect or merely sufficiently good, as unimpressive as that sounds. His standards are much broader than mine; every human he made has value. Even those who irritate us.

No one, not one person, gets front row seats in the throne-room. Remember that "neither male nor female" tidbit of scripture? That's what it means. We are all either nothing or everything, depending on your perspective, when we approach holiness.

This equality of worth puts to rest our human strivings for "success" or earthly import. Sure, it's all well and good to aim high. We must, however, sift through the difference between a quest for being a fancy-pants important person and living a life of purpose, integrity, passion, peace, and justice.

Women have value, high heavenly value, because we are borne of a promise and incubated in the glow of creative care by a God who has set us with a purpose.

We've been having this conversation for millennia. We'll be having it when I am a grandmother. There are still people who define *human* as "man." There are still women who have bought the lie. We are talking about the worth of a woman because in some countries, women are lower than second class, simply another commodity, like the milking cow or the productive goose.

But I suppose it's time to let go of my irritation and simply answer the question. The worth of a woman is exactly what God says it is. "And it was good."

Part 2: Am I Broken?

Stories of Abuse and Healing

Introduction

Tamára Lunardo

Mother's Day

The first time a man hit me,
I was not yet born,
Hid safe in her swollen belly.

She bore his temper
Until she bore me,
Her mother-heart growing her stronger.

So I never knew
The rage of his fist
Because her love was stronger than fear.

And when she left,
Battered but not broken,
She gave me a legacy of strength.

***

My mother has always been my hero. I knew she had endured much pain—physically, emotionally, spiritually—at the hands of my birth father, and I knew that it was through the strength of her love I'd been spared the same wounds. I believed in the strength she'd sown into me from the start, and I knew I would never fall victim to abuse. I was different, I was stronger, I was better.

I was wrong.

My heart was gaping with longing for the attention, acceptance, and affection I'd never had and desperately wanted from my dad, and I began to turn it, hopefully and hopelessly, to other men. I learned early and easily that you could get a man's attention, acceptance, and affection if you offered the right trade. And it seemed a fair deal—you give your body to try to soothe your soul.

I met a boy, nearly a man, in the church youth group–he was a senior, and I could hardly believe he'd pay any attention to a freshman girl. He made no secret of the fact that he was condescending to date a kid like me and took every opportunity to put me in my place. And I thought he was right—I thought this was the best I could get—so I took it because at least now I had a man's attention.

Once when I mentioned that I liked the scent of his hair, he shot back that it was his *shampoo* I liked. I shut my mouth. Another time, my little brother did something to aggravate me. My response must have had a tone of threat in it because my boyfriend grabbed a fork off the kitchen counter, backed me into a corner, and pointed the fork and his hatred straight at me. I can't remember his words, but I am certain they were stronger than the ones I had used on my brother. I didn't say another thing. Where was my mother's bravery now? Clearly not in me. But if I just kept quiet, I could earn a man's approval.

My boyfriend and I took rides around town in his secondhand sedan, often on the pretext of going on a date, but as soon as we took the turn away from town and toward the baseball field, I knew it wasn't going to be a good date for me. He would park behind the empty field, the trees dimming the bright lights that might otherwise have attracted attention. But no one saw, so no one came, and I was only fifteen. It wasn't a man's affection, but it was his physical touch, and I figured that was close enough. At least for a girl like me.

Soon, what began as pressure turned to force. One night he wanted more than I'd already given, and I didn't think I had any right to say no—I'd already been so stupid, so weak. So I didn't speak up because I didn't think I was worth speaking for, and what he forced on me that night was heavier than his large frame.

Shame and fear of disappointing my parents kept my secret locked away, and although I shared a watered down version with a few friends, no one knew the hard details or the depth of pain they caused. I was alone with my wounds, and the fear and shame they'd inflicted only made me more vulnerable.

And a pretty girl with low self-esteem is an easy target to spot, so I was hit, over and over again. Not with hands — I've never worn a man's bruise — but with force of words and of body and of shame. I failed; I was a failure. I had wounds like my mother's — they just looked different on me. I'd lost her legacy of strength and, along with my own wounds, I got a new and worse belief of my value: I was weak, and a girl who didn't have the strength to hold on to her own value probably didn't deserve it anyway.

Abuse of any kind razes the soul and sows deep lies. Victims of abuse may be in recovery all their lives — there is no simple "getting over it." As an adult I listened to a friend explain that, as long as she still had her own little ones at home, she could never adopt a child who'd been sexually abused because she knew from her father's work with sex offenders that their victims were "irreparably broken." And as I listened, I sank, because she was describing me. And the truth was I *was* broken. But her father's work had not told her the whole story. Because the truth was also that I was on the mend. I was broken, but there were, and would continue to be, repairs.

It was the strength of love that protected me from the abuse my mother suffered, and it was the strength of love that began to heal me from my own abuse. As I began years later — through counseling, family, and my own writing — to entrust each wound to the care of a God I had come to know as the Great Physician, I became a little healthier and a little stronger. With that new strength, I bared my still-healing scars for hurt friends and readers to see, and it made way for new healing for all of us. And I realized I still had my mother's legacy of strength — it just looked different on me.

The stories in this section may be difficult to read because they lay bare the most painful wounds each woman has been dealt. My mother, Julia, shows how domestic violence harms both body and soul as it creates entrapping shame, and she takes us with her on the faith journey that finally set her free. Alex uncovers the excruciating emotional pain of childhood sexual abuse and the life of sex slavery to which it led; be sure to read her bio at the end of the book to be tremendously encouraged that healing of even the deepest wounds is possible. Shanda bares the emotional wounds her father inflicted on her with physical and verbal abuse, and she bears the beautiful healing her Heavenly Father gave her with tender love. Janet reveals the deep pain of unworthiness bullying creates, worsened by the neglect of those who ought to protect and love. E.L. takes back her own story of sexual abuse and violence from her family of origin in a powerful reimagining that sets her free. Sarah exposes the damage rape, spiritual abuse, and physical violence did to her belief in her own humanity, and, with the help of healthy relationships, she boldly and beautifully reclaims it.

Whether it is evident or not in the particular parts of their stories shared here, each woman has learned that her wounds do not determine her worth. Each is a valuable, even if deeply harmed, person. Each has found healing.

There is no simple "getting over" abuse. But there is getting healthier; there is getting stronger. There is hope. Because sown deeper than even the most insidious lie is this truth: We are not our wounds.

Out of Misery and Into Joy

Julia Lunardo

The first time he hit me was on our wedding night. My husband hit me as we drove away from the reception at my parents' home to the hotel where we would spend our first night as a married couple.

I was shocked, horrified — and embarrassed. Shocked and horrified because he had never acted this way before, and I'd never been treated like that. And embarrassed because didn't these things only happen to ignorant, low-income people? My first thought was, "Oh my God! I can't stay married to this man! I need to run back into my parents' house and tell them what happened — I need to file for divorce!"

But all my friends and relatives had come to celebrate our union. Now it already appeared that our marriage was a sham. So my immediate second — and more powerful — thought was, "I can't go back and tell them what happened because my parents spent all kinds of money hosting a reception, and the guests spent their hard-earned money to buy us gifts! I made a vow til death do us part — how can I give up just hours after uttering those words?" I couldn't go back in and admit I had made a mistake.

Then the justifications started in my head: "He's never done this before — it's a fluke. He's drunk — it will never happen again."

But as most stories of domestic violence tend to go, it did happen again. Yet he was always so tearfully apologetic and tenderly loving afterward. So I forgave him, and I stayed, and the cycle continued.

One day when my husband was raging against our sweet little golden retriever puppy, Paca, she sat up straight and stared ahead as if to say, "I am not to be abused — I am to be treated with honor and respect." That made him stop in his tracks. The next time he started in on me, I remembered my puppy's lesson in dignity and worth. I imitated her defiant stance, and it worked.

That was the beginning of my awakening— the beginning of my realization that I didn't have to stay in this relationship, that I didn't have to continue to give him second and third chances. He was wrong. He was responsible for his own actions, and, although I might choose to forgive him, I was worthy of honor and respect and should not be subjected to his abuse.

Then I became pregnant. At first he was very tender with me during the pregnancy. But one day, in a drunken rage, he punched me in the stomach. *What the hell was he thinking?* I knew at that point that staying in the relationship was not an option, but I didn't know how to get out of it.

Sometimes at night when I saw a blow-up brewing, or in the midst of one, I would drive away in my car and spend hours parked on the side of the road trying to get some sleep, knowing that when I went back in the morning he would either be sober and apologetic or off to work.

My parents only lived a mile from me, but I couldn't go to them — it was just too humiliating. How could a bright and talented, college-educated woman allow herself to be in a situation like this? I felt like a failure. I felt ashamed. I felt so alone and hopeless.

Finally, when I gave birth to my beautiful and perfect baby girl, I worked up the courage to leave. As I looked into her innocent and trusting baby-blue eyes, I knew that I could never subject her to a life with this man. So far he had been loving and gentle with her, but I could not trust that that would continue. I might not have felt worthy enough to leave him for my own sake, but I had to leave him for hers. Although I couldn't yet claim it for myself, she was indeed worthy and valuable enough. She gave me courage and resolve.

I finally told my family. My parents and brothers stood up for me and my baby, helping to get us out of his house for good so that she would never know his angry outbursts and abuse and I would endure them no longer.

The gift of my daughter's life sent me back to church to give thanks to the God of my youth, whom I had put on the back burner. It made me want to rediscover Him and to re-establish a relationship with Him.

During my pregnancy I feared that, due to my sin and unworthiness, God might punish me by causing me to lose my baby or by causing me to give birth to one with severe medical problems. I was amazed and humbled to discover that He doesn't work that way — He is gracious and merciful. He joyfully heaps blessings upon His children even when they don't deserve it.

In going back to church, in hearing the Word of God, in relearning about the life, ministry, sacrifice, death, and resurrection of Jesus Christ, I began to understand God's love and amazing grace. For a while, though, I couldn't get myself to go up to the altar to receive Communion. I wasn't quite ready to accept such an awesome gift.

Gradually I began to comprehend that by being created in the image of God—by being His child—I was someone of worth. It took me a while, but I began to understand that the way I saw the beauty, and inherent dignity, and worth of my daughter was the same way my God saw me. That's when I was finally able to allow myself to receive the sacrament of Holy Communion—I was worthy to commune with God because He'd made me so.

My faith journey continues, and it has enabled me to forgive my abuser. It has even allowed me to be thankful for him because in the mysterious, hazel eyes of my daughter, in her clear and pure soprano voice, in the way she uses words to express herself so beautifully, I see glimpses of the man I once loved. However, though she may have inherited some of his characteristics and talents, she is not his—nor mine for that matter. She is uniquely and powerfully her own, and she is—most importantly—His.

Decades later I still struggle with my sense of worth and my self-confidence. The domestic violence coupled with other negative life experiences makes achieving a sense of worthiness a continuous journey. But, thanks to a dignified dog, a precious baby, a supportive family, and the amazing love and grace of my Lord, I am able to continue that journey out of misery and into joy.

Who Told You That You Were Naked?

Alex

In third grade, a group of us girls sat in a circle outside at recess and listened as a good little Catholic girl told us the "facts" about sex. She told us that sex was when a man put his penis into a woman's vagina.

After all of the squeals of disgust and declarations of "Ew! That's gross!" she went on to explain that until a woman had sex, she was a virgin, and good girls stayed virgins until they got married. They wore a white dress when they got married because they were still pure. And girls who lost their virginity before getting married were dirty sluts who were going to burn in Hell.

As the conversation went on around me, I felt as if time had stopped. There was so much heat burning inside of me, I was sure the world had stopped spinning and was falling into the sun. The sound of my blood pounding in my ears was so loud, I just knew all of them could hear it. I became very still, terrified that if I moved a muscle, if I even breathed, they would see — they would know.

They would know that I had already lost my virginity — long before I knew what it was or that in order to be a good girl, I was supposed to keep it.

Because since I was five years old, my daddy had been putting his penis in my vagina at night. I hadn't known that it was called "sex." I only knew that it hurt and I didn't like it and I wanted him to stop, but he said he had to do it.

I did know I wasn't supposed to talk about it. My mother had taught me that.

The morning after the first time it happened—that horrible, painful first time when I thought he was killing me, when it felt like he was tearing me in pieces—there was a lot of blood on my sheets. I watched as my mother stripped the bed and put them in the washing machine, and I waited for her to ask about the blood. But she said nothing.

She said nothing about my funny walk as I hobbled to the living room to watch cartoons. She said nothing that night as she put me in the tub for my bath and I bit my fingers, fighting back sobs as the water hit the place I was torn and burned me like fire.

She said nothing—and so I choked back my cries, and I said nothing too.

So I knew I didn't like it, I knew it hurt, and I knew I shouldn't speak of it—but until that moment at recess, I hadn't known that I was dirty and would burn in Hell. Every time after my father left my bed, I would curl up crying, and I would feel God wrap His arms around me and hold me until I fell asleep. I knew that God loved me. But the heat of shame that invaded me that day on the playground began to melt the edges of my faith. How could God love me if I was a dirty slut?

I knew my daddy loved me. I thought what he did to me was a part of that love—the painful, icky part you had to suffer through to get the good part. I knew because every time as he pushed into me over and over, he would rhythmically tell me, "Daddy - loves - you - Daddy - loves - you - Daddy - loves…" And then there would be a present brought home the next day, and he would be nice to me for a few days. And if I did something wrong, he wouldn't even punch me for it like he usually did.

So I learned that love came with a price that required a sacrifice of pain. That to be valuable to my father meant allowing him to use my body however he wanted. And when the special attention my favorite uncle showed me turned into his making me give him a blow job at age twelve, I learned that that was my value to other men as well.

As the years passed and my pleadings to God to make it stop went unanswered, I grew angry. I didn't just want Him to comfort me anymore—I wanted Him to stop the pain. And so I ran away from home, from God—out of His arms, away from my pain.

And the knowledge of where my worth lay was confirmed by many, many more men. My body was the only thing of value I possessed to trade for the things I needed to survive. I allowed men to take what they wanted from me, and they would give me what I needed in return. I learned all the ways to give men pleasure, and I learned all the ways to numb the pain in my soul.

Yet, secretly, I was searching for rescue. Every time a man came to me, I hoped that he would see me as something more than a piece of meat to act out his fantasy upon. That he would sweep me up out of the filth and tell me I deserved a better life. That he would tell me I was beautiful and didn't have to be a whore anymore. That he would love me and take care of me.

It never happened. A few men were nicer than others, just using me to alleviate their own loneliness. But most were perverted in what gave them pleasure and used me for things they would never dare to do to their wives or girlfriends. After all, I was a child, with a child's body—and men who desire sex with children are not men with "healthy" sexual appetites. A few were purely evil and took sadistic pleasure in inflicting pain upon me.

But whether they were nice or evil, I was the same to all of them. I was a piece of merchandise to be bought and used however they wished. I was never a person to any of them—I was just a whore.

What did the world teach me I was worth?

About $10 to $30, depending on what you wanted.

Of Tears and Healing

Shanda Sargent

In love's service, only wounded soldiers can serve. –Thornton Wilder

Fists tight, he pounded on the door roaring for me to let him enter. The walls rattled. Fear iced my blood. I was trapped.

Alone. Nowhere to run. No one to rescue me.

If I screamed, no one would hear. His anger punished the door with more blows. If I didn't unlock the door, his rage would deepen and erupt like a volcano spewing uncontrollably. No doubt, he would crush the door. I submissively obeyed. Shaking, I turned the lock on the knob. He bulldozed the door, and in a flash I was slammed up against the wall, his hands around my neck, strangling me, my feet dangling off the ground. His green eyes blazed with sparks of fire. Spit curled on his tongue and sprayed my face—every word grunted through his clenched, nicotine-stained teeth.

Alone. Nowhere to run. No one to rescue me.

He'd threatened to kill me many times before. I knew this would be the day. But from somewhere down deep, I decided to look death in the face. If I was going to die at his hands, he was going to have the memory of piercing eyes staring into him while he murdered. As I stared, he cursed words I didn't even know. His grip around my neck tightened as he shoved me farther up the wall, then miraculously, his fingers released. I was in disbelief. *He let go.* I took a moment to gather myself. I slipped past him, grabbed my book bag, ladled a small cup of courage from a well that had always been out of reach, turned to him, jaw set, and said,

"If you ever lay a hand on me again, I'm calling the police, and you can rot in jail." Fighting tears that threatened to burst a faulty dam, I darted out the door and ran to the end of the driveway.

Alone. Nowhere to run. No one to rescue me.

We lived in the middle of a corn field. I hoped and prayed Big Yellow #19 would arrive a little early. I kept looking towards the house. Would he dart outside to finish me off? I paced back and forth the narrow end of the drive to pass the longest five minutes of my life. When the accordion door of the school bus opened, I realized for the first time in my seventeen years that I had risen victorious from being his victim, if only for a brief moment.

I shamefully looked down as I got on the bus so the driver wouldn't notice that I was emotionally rattled. I was the first passenger on the bus, and there would be a seven-minute window before the next student boarded. The driver had always been kind to me — should I tell her what just happened? Could she help? Or would my asking for help get back to him and backfire? If it did, he would kill both my mom and me. There would be no miraculous release of fingers, to be certain. It was too risky. I quietly sank into my place in the very last seat, bravery collapsed. Silent tears washed away the next few miles. Surrounded by tall, green vinyl seats, I was safe. The rattle of the bus heater hummed a strange yet familiar peace, and I quickly applied makeup to hide my sorrow before the next riders boarded the bus. I packed away the morning's events with all the other baggage he had given me to lug and I went to class.

Alone. Nowhere to run. No one to rescue me.

*Even though I walk through the valley of the **shadow of death**... You are with me. –Psalm 23:4*

His life was broken on the back of alcohol, and in turn he broke mine. Little girls should not be physically forced to chug down warm beer from their father's stein for his own amusement. A daughter should be adored. Young girls should not have to empty soup pots full of their father's hangover-induced vomit. A daughter should be cherished. Young women should not have to endure demeaning comments about who they are, what they look like, and what they do. A daughter should be strengthened and praised.

A daughter should be wanted, treasured, and enjoyed. There were no piggy back rides, tickling games, or bedtime stories; he didn't teach me how to throw a ball, build with blocks, or ride a bicycle. A father's eyes should sparkle and dance when his daughter enters the room. My presence made him seethe, and he controlled me with his rage. Small girls should climb into their father's laps, safe, and in their strong arms be hugged and cuddled. The gentleness of a father's touch was unknown to me, and his wrath ruled our home.

Broken girl. Splintered heart. Fractured soul.

I was six years old. Intimidation crippled me. I stood frozen while he forcibly pinned my mother's hand to the kitchen counter. She was crying desperately, begging for mercy. His tongue gushed venom. He grabbed a squatty drinking glass from the decorative brass holder. Pretty green flowers and vines were etched on the set of eight. I had always admired them. Swiftly, he took one of the glasses and slammed it down on my mother's hand. Broken flower shards flew across the counter. Terror wilted my heart. Years later, the brass holder still remained on the counter with seven glasses instead of eight— a constant, gaping reminder of the one I should not cross.

Broken girl. Splintered heart. Fractured soul.

He was in the basement. He called me downstairs to assist in a project, like all the others he'd started but would never finish. As I hopped off the final step, he suddenly threw a 1960s oval rotary telephone at me. This was the same treasured telephone I used to play "house" with. The toy-turned-weapon pummeled my thighs and its curly blue cord entangled my feet. I stumbled and fell. He laughed. I quickly and carefully unwound myself from the cord web, limped upstairs to my room, locked the door, and hid deep in my closet under my pink fuzzy blanket to cry. I was longing to be found, but not by him.

Broken girl. Splintered heart. Fractured soul.

*The LORD is close to the **brokenhearted**; he rescues those whose **spirits are crushed**. –Psalm 34:18*

The presence of violence, anger, and abuse robbed me of my worth, damaged my being, and saddled me with baggage beyond my own carrying; the absence of tenderness, kindness, encouragement, and love left a cavernous hole in my heart; together, these forces firmly affixed lies to my soul. Insecurity ravaged me. I built walls. I hid the broken girl behind a perfected appearance. I was sensitive and tender to a fault. I sought approval with boys, which created more baggage. I limped along. I survived.

Wounds and sorrow.

After nineteen years of prison, I was out. I'd done my time. I was free. But I was only free in the sense that I was away from him. A near-perfect man married broken me, swooped me away from my fractured home, and in return I dumped my luggage in his lap—heavy, massive luggage. Two naïve nineteen-year-olds began life together toting burdens and forging through.

Wounds and sorrow.

For the first time in my life, I was safe. For the first time in my life, I was nurtured. For the first time in my life, I was rescued. Yet, the compassion and tenderness from a loving husband didn't calm the raging waves of insecurity. His strong and gentle presence didn't silence the nightmares that left me heaving in sobs and screaming out in fear. His calm demeanor and wise words couldn't heal my gaping soul.

Wounds and sorrow.

*He **heals** the brokenhearted and **binds up their wounds**. –Psalm 147:3 NIV*

I was thirty-three years old. We had just experienced a deep loss in our family, and my wounded heart could not sustain its walled fortress that normally protected soul-deep places. I was soaking in a bubble bath and drowning in tears. The sorrow of my broken-girl past rushed to the surface. In that moment, the suffering inflicted by my own father became too much to bear. Praying and weeping, pleading and agonizing, I was crumbling under the pain of my past, which was now intertwined with the brokenness of my present. Then in a sacred moment beyond words, He came to me. He came and pierced my sorrow.

Tears and healing.

God met me in the bathtub, and the bathtub, of all places, became holy ground. He whispered deep into the bones of my soul. In a crazy-miraculous way, I heard His voice:

> *Shanda, I was there. I was with you. Every tear you cried, every ache you felt, every wound inflicted – I was there. Every humiliation, every defeat, and every sorrow – I was with you. I hurt when you hurt. I cried when you cried. I want you to know that I'm sorry. I'm sorry for what you went through, but you were not alone, and you are not alone now.*

Tears and healing.

His words lifted baggage. His words mended me in soothing grace. I saw God's heart for me. I was His daughter – His little girl. For the first time, my father's lies were being silenced by my Father's Truth.

Tears and healing.

You keep track of all my sorrows. You have **collected all my tears in your bottle***. You have recorded each one in your book. –Psalm 56:8*

A river of tears and pain became a river of healing. Wounds became scars. Even though I'd known Him almost my entire life, for the first time, chains fell and I trusted Him. I surrendered my walled fortress at the Cross. I looked back with newfound clarity on my life and saw drops of providence on my path. In freedom's healing, my ugly story became beautiful – a beautiful grace.

True purpose. True worth.

Without experiencing real pain, one cannot have true compassion. Having walked the road of an abuser's daughter, I empathize with those who have a similar path. My sensitive heart feels deeply. Instead of broken pieces, these are now beautiful gifts. These experiences have gifted me to be who I am. Deep in my soul bones, I know that I am His little girl.

True purpose. True worth.

I know He loves me, and it is His eyes that dance when I walk in the room. Now, every single drop of my worth is filtered first through His crazy, head-over-heels Father-love. I know He allowed me to experience the rawness of pain and suffering so that I could become a wounded healer.[3] If my broken story can touch just one; if just one damaged girl will hear Truth and soak into her soul that she is His little girl, too; if she can experience His deep want and love for her, then my journey will have added redemption.

True purpose. True worth.

Wounded healers remain somewhat broken. I still struggle sometimes, and I still feel twinges of pain from my past, but it keeps me connected to who I am and why I am. Wounds salved by grace, mercy, love, and Jesus inspire my passion to love those around me. Now I know my worth. I am His.

True purpose. True worth.

*How **great is the love** the Father has lavished on us, that we should be called **Children of God**! And **that is what we are**! –1 John 3:1*

---

3   The concept of "wounded healer" has many sources, but my understanding of it comes from Henri J. M. Nouwen's *The Wounded Healer* (Doubleday 1979).

The Unwanted

Janet Heath

It goes back as far as I can remember. Born just 13 months after my sister, I was a mistake—nobody wanted or was prepared for me. I screamed my way through the first six months of my life, and I have cried my way through the rest of it. I grew up being bullied by my sister, unwanted by my mother, and unloved by my father.

My mother tried with me as much as she had to, but her health issues physically limited her. My father doted on my sister; she was his cohort in crime. And when my brother came along five years after me, he was not considered a mistake. By that time, my mother had had a partial hysterectomy and her doctors had told her she would never conceive again; he was a "miracle from God." So she treated my brother as "my Son, my Son, my only Son, with whom I am well pleased."

Since my mother spent a lot of time in the hospital, we kids were farmed out to family members for months at a time. My sister was always with our paternal grandmother, who affectionately called her "kitten." But my brother and I didn't exist to her, so our paternal aunt took in my brother; I was the last one placed.

My loving godmother-aunt took me in each time even though she had five children. She treated me as one of her own, as she lined us all up in the hallway every night for bedtime, like an assembly line: wash, dry, p.j.'s, story, bed. I was the same age as my cousin, so I slept in her bed with her, wore her extra school uniform, and sat in her seat with her at school. But I felt like I was my cousin's shadow. I was just… there. Never made a peep.

When we got a bit older, we just stayed home alone. My sister and I were well-taught in the household chores — we did all the cooking, cleaning, and ironing (pure cotton shirts, standing on a step stool) and took care of our baby brother. But my sister was a mean one — she took up the mantle of eldest with relish and doled out daily beatings along with threats of death if we told on her.

Sometimes she would hit me in the back so hard I couldn't breathe and thought I would die. (Of course, I never did; I just cried. I cried my way through childhood, it seems.) If she left marks on me, she would make me lie about them. My brother would tell on her all the time, and my sister would get in trouble for hitting him — the precious one — so she eventually turned all her attention on me. One time she hit me over the head with a big glass whiskey bottle, and it shattered and cut her foot so badly that she had to go get stitches — she blamed me, of course. She tortured me every day of my life until I left home and went to college.

When my mother wasn't in the hospital, she worked and then came home and went straight to bed. If we woke her up from our "goofing around" — which typically consisted of my running away from my sister, screaming — my mother would come out of her bedroom in a rage and slap me across the face and tell me to shut up. I always did. I would have without the slap. But if I tried to explain, my mother would just slap me again.

If we were really bad, she would go get my father's belt. We knew we were in big trouble then. My sister would just run out the front door, slamming it in my face so I couldn't escape. My brother would go hide in his bed, but he was never in any danger. This would leave me to get all the punishment and rage my mother had built up. During one such beating, the buckle of the belt hit me in the face and split my lip open and blackened my eye. Blood was spurting everywhere, which just made me scream louder, and this made my mother angrier. My sister came back in and stood there laughing at me while I was literally being beaten bloody. My mother just blamed me for making her so angry that she drew blood.

My father never said a word. If he knew about any of this, he never mentioned it. He was not at all a hands-on dad—he worked, came home, ate dinner, and snored on the couch until bedtime. He never laid a hand on us, just called us "rotten kids." I can't remember him ever talking to me one-on-one, or hugging me, or saying, "I love you."

But for all the darkness of home, school was one place where I could shine. My teachers appreciated me; I was a model student and got straight A's. I was never praised at home for my grades, though, because my sister always got C's and below, and my parents didn't want to make her feel bad by praising me. Still, I loved school. I was not the most popular, but I had real friends. I even made the junior high cheerleading squad, much to my surprise and my sister's dismay, as she had failed in her quest the year before. My success just enraged her even more.

We both had certain chores to be done every day before our mother came home from work. Because I had cheerleading practice after school, I missed the bus, so I had to walk home about three miles every day, even in winter. But I didn't walk—I ran so I would be home in time to do my chores. Even so, my sister maliciously made sure I would fail. She would purposely mess everything up so there would be no way I could finish in time, knowing that I would be punished for it. She hated me because I was a cheerleader, and she made me pay dearly for it.

I never even bothered to try out in high school. It required far too much commitment from both the student and the parents; I knew I could never keep up with my home chores, and my parents only cared about my brother's sports, not mine. But I still excelled in my studies and got straight A's. Meanwhile, my sister spent most of her time in high school skipping school or sleeping in the nurse's office. Once again, it made no difference to my parents—there was no reward for Gold honor roll.

When I was a junior, we moved. My sister said she no longer wanted to share a bedroom with me, so I was relegated to the basement. I had a twin bed and a dresser behind a small screen in the family room. My father would stay up until two o'clock every night watching TV because he napped every evening after dinner. I would beg him to turn off the TV so I could go to sleep but to no avail—I was in *his* family room. So I didn't get much sleep, but at least I didn't have to worry about my sister throwing things at me in the middle of the night.

That same year, I told my mother I wanted to go to college. She said I didn't need to go—I should just study shorthand and typing so I could be a secretary, like her. When I pushed back and said I wanted to be a teacher, she said they could not afford to send me to college. But according to the bank that I went to for a loan, they could afford it; still I got nothing, as they would not co-sign for me.

So I started working at the burger joint down the street from the high school. I had so many credits already, I only had to go to school half days. I would go to school at eight, walk to my job at noon, work until ten or eleven, and then walk home. I did this until I graduated. During the summers I worked full-time during the week as a secretary and at the burger joint on nights and weekends. I saved up enough money for two years of college. When I got to college, I immediately got a full-time job there—I took a full load of classes and worked 40 hours a week.

But I was free. No sister beating the shit out of me every day. No mother beating me with a belt because of my sister. No bed in the basement. I loved college! I came home the first few holidays but then just decided to stay at school and work, even over the summers. By then I was living in a sorority house and could stay there year-round. I was Social Chairman and a social butterfly— everybody loved me and I loved them. Finally, I had a home and a family.

But my sister got jealous that I was at college while she had to work as a bank teller. So my mother forced me to come home from college one weekend and take the college entrance tests for my sister. I told her that if I got caught, I would get kicked out of school. She didn't care; she just wanted my sister to be able to go to college, no matter the consequences for me. Luckily, at the last minute, my sister decided not to go—she knew she was not college material.

After college, I spent six months at home. My mother insisted I pay rent right away, and she had a full-time job lined up for me the day I got home. I was never allowed to sleep in on weekends or read books; my sister and I still had to do all the chores. She got married that spring, and my parents paid for her lavish wedding. I was glad she was leaving, but then that left all the chores to me. When the servitude inevitably got worse, I decided to leave for good too.

I got married in the fall, but my parents told me that they had no money to give me for a wedding, that they had spent all they had on my sister. But I didn't want or need their money. I paid for my own wedding.

We just wanted to elope, but my mother forced us to have a "proper" wedding and reception just like my sister — because what would the relatives think if I didn't have a big affair like hers? But my mother insisted that no one know that I paid for it. So I had to go through with the whole farce of a proper wedding I didn't even want, at my own expense. It was all about appearances for my mother; I was just glad to be gone.

My father died shortly thereafter, and my mother gave my sister and brother inheritance money under the pretense that they needed it and I didn't. It goes back as far as I can remember. I was never their child. I was a mistake — no one wanted me.

Reckoning Day

E.L. Farris

Little El sits really still and doesn't move. He hunts her. They are coming. If I were there with her now, with the rest of her family hovering over her and screaming at her, maybe I would finally say all the things she buried and stuffed inside.

The best times in my childhood were the ones I spent hoping and dreaming for something better to happen. I never lived in the moment because the moments hurt too much. I dreamed of a different life in a place where I felt safe; I roamed through galaxies and across oceans and skipped over decades and leaped forward into the creases of a future I could never make come alive. The miracle is not so much that I made it to the here and now — the miracle is that I made that future come alive.

And there is something I need to take care of for little El. I need to travel back and provide a reckoning. And this time, I write the story. This time, I speak for little El and protect her, and while it's just a fantasy, the child inside me needs this. She needs a reckoning.

Big El walks into the new house and little El runs to greet her. In the split-second before they hug, the adult body transmogrifies with a successive, cascading version of little Els, until younger versions of me rejoin and reunite inside of me. I am little El and big El and I carry her easily inside of me and when I breathe, she does too. *I got you now, little El, and if you need to talk, I will say it for you. They can't touch you anymore.* I feel her relax and lay her head on my shoulder and I know she's staring at my weathered boots. Yep, still got them. It's ass-kicking time.

I'm three years old and my hair tumbles over my shoulder. My bathing suit is red, white, and blue. I hate the sand. Someone shoves a finger under my bathing suit and I don't know who it is but I kick him in the head and run, yelling like a German warrior princess, into the ocean's welcoming arms.

I'm four and Mom sends me upstairs to give Dad a massage and hands me funky tools from the kitchen. I glare at her and throw the sex toys right back at her. One of them hits her face and she cries in shock, "What did you do that for?" Over my shoulder I yell, "Don't pretend you don't know, you fucking idiot." And I slam the door behind me.

Dad lies on the bed waiting for me, and I laugh at the green bedspread. He waits and I break his whiskey bottle over his head. "The priest I talked to said that you need to ask God to forgive you. It's above my pay grade, apparently. And here's an extra blow to your head for the weird stirring I feel in my vagina. Y'all are the ones who created the synaptic connection between getting turned on sexually and people hurting me."

I'm five. I take Barbie away from Tonto and the Lone Ranger. They are raping her and I won't stand for it. "Boys, don't touch my doll. If you can't play nice, you can't play in my home," and I ceremoniously cut their heads off and throw them into the trashcan. They're lucky I did not quarter them. Quartering hurts more but I don't believe in torture.

I'm eleven. This neighborhood boy struts past me and stares at my breasts through my white blouse. "Ooh, boobs," he exclaims, and reaches out to grab them. Before he lays a hand on me, I cold-cock him in the head and knock him to the ground. "No," I insist, swatting his hand away. "You better study harder in college because your NFL career will only last four years. Oh, and remember what your coach will yell at you when you drop easy passes: 'NFL stands for Not For Long if you can't hold on to the ball.'"

I'm eleven still. I smell Dad's whiskey and hear the ice cubes tinkling in his Manhattan glass. He motions for me to sit on his lap and when I do, he runs his hand over my breasts. I reach over to the lamp table where his drink rests and pour it over his head and punch him in the face. "Don't ever touch me again, you sick, drunk bastard," I yell, and I run out of the house and never stop.

I'm twelve. I get drunk the night before and pass out in the basement. That is when the rape occurs, and it may have taken me years to piece this together and I still doubt the shattered shards of images, but the blood and the aching in my loins don't lie. I sit on the porch retching and my demon-mom is screaming at the top of her lungs, "You little bitch! You slut! How could you do this? I hate you! You make me sick, you little bitch, and now you will run and keep running until I say you can stop."

She grabs her bicycle and I stride over to her and slap her upside the head as hard as I can. And with super-human strength I throw her copper-colored Schwinn. It levitates and flies higher and higher until it breaks into as many pieces as my soul once was in.

And then I stalk toward her and in a measured voice I state, "You failed me. You failed me over and over. You want to know why I took my love and held it tightly inside me, where you could not access it? Because you are unworthy of me and everything that I am and was and will be. I never asked to be raped and molested. No girl ever asks for it.

And stop crying. For once this isn't about you. This is my story and you need to get your sick self back in the house and leave me alone. Go hunt down your son or your husband and figure out who did this to me and get me the help I need. Don't ship me off to summer camp tomorrow morning. Don't pretend everything is okay and pat yourself on the back for holding this shitbox of a family together. This is your chance and if you fail me now, you failed me forever."

I'm all different ages and Dad leers at me and grabs my ass and I take my elbow and whack him in the nose. Blood flows down and I hiss, "Leave me the hell alone." My brother punches me over and over and I grab a hammer from the garage and take it to him. He yelps in pain and screams, "But you made me do it! It's your fault I beat you every day." I shake my head and reply, "You will become a drunk just like your father. Have fun with that."

I'm fifteen and yet again Mom launches into an hour-long tirade. Instead of tuning out the jaded speech and storing it in my brain to listen to on auto-replay, I jump out of bed and argue with her ferociously. "You stupid bitch," she screams. "Bullshit. I have a 145 IQ." She stares at me in shock, and then she continues, "You're an ungrateful piece of shit and you're fat and you're going to end up working at K-Mart and never amount to anything."

I laugh at her angrily. "No, Mom. I graduate from William and Mary Law School with top grades. I represent some of the largest corporations in the country and earn $145,000 a year until I get pregnant with my children—the very same ones you will tell me not to have. I have them and I love them, and it's kind of ironic because the one thing you said I could do, write fiction, is what I'm doing now. But I don't write for you or for Dad or for anyone. I write for the same reason a bird sings: because I have to and I love to and I must and no one, nothing, can take that away from me, not even you." With that last retort I grab her by the shoulder, fling my door open, and in a booming voice cry out, "Now get the hell out of my room and stay out!"

I'm eighteen. My brother is home from college and I'm wearing tight Guess jeans and I'd trade a few years off the end of my life to have that lithe body back, right up until the time he throws me down on the sofa and climbs on top of me. I cannot move and his dick is pressing into me and it hurts through my jeans and I don't know what to do... but wait, yes I do.

"Get off! Get off me or I swear to God I am going to kill you." I fight back with all I have and that is when his girlfriend walks into the room, and his eyes get all luminous and he lets me go and grabs her and starts to grind into her instead of me. I don't walk out of the room. I give him a boot to the head and as he examines the tread marks I've left, I glare at his future wife and say, "He's a sick pervert. Didn't you see what he was doing to me? Do you really want to give up your career as a rocket scientist for an alcoholic asshole? And, brother, you had better hope there are no unsolved crimes in our neighborhood."

I'm twenty-five. I keep having rape nightmares and when I tell Mom, I don't accept her response. She says, "Well, your brother always was a horny bastard, but I don't remember him doing anything like that to you," and instead of staring at the phone and acquiescing silently, I say, "Bullshit. You let us sleep together. You sent me up to give Dad massages. You knew what happened the night I was raped and you blamed me. You hit me and screamed at me and abused the hell out of me, all of you, and now you're too much of a coward to face it. Just know this: I know what all of you did. And I will pray that you find a reckoning for your sins."

I'm thirty-two. My daughter is six months old. We're visiting my parents' house and Mom volunteers to change her diaper. Dad watches and then he says in front of my husband and in front of me, "Wow, she is gorgeous. She reminds me of an angel in a centerfold." My husband and I stare at one another in shock. I have told him about the flashbacks and dreams and jigsaw puzzle-like memories that inhabit my brain, but it doesn't click until he hears my father speak these chilling words. But instead of laughing uncomfortably and asking myself if I heard it correctly, I know what to do this time. I take my daughter and leave and I do not look back. They hurt me, but I am a woman now, and I can protect my own daughter. I can protect myself.

It's the present day. My hands are shaking and it feels like a freight train crashed through my private parts but I am safe here, and so is little El. This is my story and today is my reckoning day. And it was a long time coming. I am a woman now and I am strong enough to tell a story that needed to be told.

I Am Human

Sarah Moon

I was born human.

But I was also born female.

The simple fact of my femaleness placed my humanity in jeopardy from the start. It would not be long—not long at all—before I first questioned my humanity. It would not be long before men, with their objectifying glances, greedy hands, and dehumanizing words would steal that humanity from me. No, it was not long at all. I was only six.

Six.

I still thought that boys had cooties and that mommies and daddies prayed together when they wanted a baby and that Jesus put the baby in the mommies' tummies. I wasn't ready to learn the things that I learned that spring day in my church's nursery.

He was my cousin. He was ten years older than me. And one Sunday, when everyone else in the church was enjoying a potluck dinner in the fellowship hall, he took me upstairs to the nursery to play. We played house.

"You're the mommy. I'm the daddy," he said. "This is what mommies and daddies do."

And I tried to fight but he was bigger.

I carried the images of that day with me: the blankets of the nursery crib, covered in rabbits, each dressed in a marching band uniform and playing a musical instrument; the sound of footsteps below that I prayed would come my way; and those ice-cold fingers.

But clearer in my mind than any of these was the feeling that I was a toy. That my cousin had plucked me from the nursery toy box to touch me, handle me, play with me. I never forgot that feeling, and I spent the remainder of my childhood feeling quite inhuman.

Then, there was the pastor.

I was thirteen—still young, insecure, and impressionable, body parts changing and new desires emerging. And I was at church camp, sitting through yet another uncomfortable sermon in the hot, crowded chapel, the smell of sweat and pine hanging in the air.

The pastor preached on Song of Solomon, and I vigorously took notes and highlighted my Bible like a good Baptist. The night before, the other girls in my cabin and I had stayed up late, reading Song of Solomon and giggling at the intimacy therein that we did not yet understand. But none of us were giggling now.

The yelling I was used to—I was raised Fundamental Baptist, after all. But the words coming from the pastor's red face were frightening.

"You young women!" he screamed, "You listen to what Song of Solomon says: 'Thou art all fair, my love; there is no spot in thee.' There was no spot in this woman. No flaws. She was perfect and pure, and that's why her husband thought she was beautiful."

He continued, "If you don't save your virginity for your husbands, you won't be pure anymore, and no good Christian man will find you beautiful. He will look at you and see only the filth that you've done."

I sat in fear. Because I knew I wasn't a virgin.

And the yelling went on: "Would you young men buy an ugly, dented-up car that someone had already crashed into a wall? Would you brush your teeth with a toothbrush that some other man had already gotten his slobber all over? Would you eat a sandwich that someone had chewed up and spat back out?"

Again, my humanity—squashed beneath those objectifying words. I felt that I was not a woman, but a banged-up, used car; a spit-covered toothbrush; a chewed-up sandwich. It didn't matter that

I had been stolen. It didn't matter that I had not asked to be spit upon or chewed up. I was an object that could depreciate in value. A broken toy that no one would ever want to play with again.

So when a man finally did show interest in me, I jumped at the opportunity to be loved, feeling that this opportunity might be my only one. My friends told me I could do better, but they didn't know. They didn't know that I was a broken toy on the shelf of a second-hand store. They didn't know, like I did, that I was dating the only man my used body could afford.

But he knew, the man I met at age sixteen. And he told me so at every opportunity.

"You're lucky I'm so forgiving," he'd say. "No one else would want you because you're damaged goods. You can't do any better than me."

But he tried to fix me. When he saw a flaw, he'd cover it with a bruise. When he saw a dent, he'd hammer it out with words that pounded on my soul and shattered my spirit.

And when he used me like a toy, like my cousin had done so many years before, I did not object because, as he reminded me, he had other toys that he could be playing with. As he held my head down, I held back the tears. Even as I choked on his semen and vomited in my mouth, I tried to swallow like he told me to because I didn't want to be thrown out, even more broken than before.

But he threw me out anyway. When he left, he called me worthless. He told me I didn't deserve him. I cried and begged for him to stay, even though I hated him, because if I wasn't even good enough for a monster like him, then who was I good enough for?

I'm not exactly sure how I escaped all the objectifying lies from my past and found my humanity again, but now I'm twenty-two and I am sure of this: I am not a broken toy. Not a used car or an old toothbrush or a half-eaten sandwich. But a woman. And a human.

My journey back to humanity has been a rocky one, but there were landmarks along the way that I recall, like the meeting with my youth pastor and his wife where I spilled my story out in desperate tears and where I first heard the words, "It wasn't your fault." The Bible study group where I shared my story among several other women, and they shared their stories, and we hugged, and there were so many painful but beautiful tears, and, oh, how many tissues we went through. The boyfriend (now fiancé) who saw not brokenness, but strength; who loved me not as a toy, but as an equal—as a human. The feminist group where I joined my sisters in the fight against female objectification.

Somewhere, between sixteen and twenty-two, I became a human again. Now I wear the title proudly. I am Sarah Moon; I am a woman.

And I am human.

Part 3: Am I Visible?

Stories of Society and Culture

Introduction

Tamára Lunardo

A Sacrifice to All the Wrong Gods

Some days I believe
I am more
When there is less of me,
That my words
Bear more weight
When I bear it less,
That my deeds
Tip scales
When I don't.
And untruths
Are easy to buy
When I am feeling cheap,
So I bring plates
Filled with lies
As fragrant offerings,
And make myself
A sacrifice
To all the wrong gods.

***

With all the things a teenager has to worry about, I thanked God at least I was thin. I was a dancer all my life, and I had the naturally long, lean frame of a ballerina. So I didn't worry a whole lot about my body — I knew boys liked it, and that was good enough. Maybe I was good enough.

But I could tell I was different from a lot of the other girls at my upper-middle-class high school. For one, I was lower-middle-class. They got new cars for their birthdays; I got to borrow my dad's used car with a power steering fluid leak. But I didn't care — I loved driving that old red convertible with the top down. I felt free.

And I felt free to be different, to wear my Goodwill, plaid old man pants and tiny tank tops while the other girls wore khaki skirts and polo shirts, to streak my hair blue while they highlighted theirs blond, to hang out with gay kids and theater geeks while they dated jocks and jockeyed for popularity, to speak up when I disagreed with a teacher while they quietly earned teacher's pet. I felt free to be myself, but I felt that freedom come at a price.

They had a name for kids like me in the nineties: freaks. It didn't have a pejorative sense on the surface — it was just another social label. But I was a smart student, and I understood what my quirkiness meant to the other girls. I would be tolerated in spite of my real self, but I would never match, never fit in, never belong. I would never be accepted *because* of my real self.

I was in my high school's dance group, and my senior year, I had the opportunity to audition to become an officer or even the principal dancer. I had dreamed of becoming principal dancer since I was a freshman. I knew I had the chops. Some of the other girls had had a few years of dance lessons here and there, but I had grown up in a dance studio — I had been well trained in classical ballet since I was two. I moved easily up the levels at my dance studio, and my teachers encouraged me that, if I wanted to put in the effort, they thought I had the kind of talent to become a professional ballerina. But at school, principal dancer was determined by peer vote. I didn't even get officer. If I wouldn't play by their rules, I could still play, but no way in hell could I win.

I didn't want to try to fit myself into anyone else's mold because I knew how uncomfortable it would make me. But you cannot go on for long, resisting a mold that everyone else seems to fit so well, before wondering whether the reason you don't fit is that you are, in fact, misshapen. I desperately needed to be myself, and I hated that that self was so nonhomogeneous. I was angry at myself for being so stubbornly, inherently *other*, and I was angry at the world for finding my other-ness unacceptable. And so I built a defense of pissed-off protection so no one would see — least of all, me — that there was really something wrong with me, and I raged against the machine until it let me loose. But when I finally got out of high school for the wide-open freedom of college, I found that the machine was still up and running — and it was making me another mold.

I was no longer dancing and I suddenly had to cook for myself with only a microwave and a hotplate; right on schedule, I began gaining the Freshman Fifteen. I would walk across campus to class and notice all sorts of people. I relaxed with the realization that somewhere between the grungy hippy girl in the theater department and the dapper boy in the music school, I'd be able to be my real self. But as I traversed the campus, I also noticed that other girls' thighs didn't touch at the top, and that seemed even more beautiful than any real me could ever be.

The sorority girl in the neighboring dorm room was the skinniest person I had ever seen in real life. She reminded me of photos I'd seen of Holocaust victims, but she wore a plastic smile and a bleached hairdo and an overwhelming condescension. She paraded her birth control pack like a reward for best behavior, and she rolled the names of fancy foods off her tongue so well I almost believed she ate them. She was so nearly adult and so nearly perfect. I might have wanted to become friends with her or to become her, except that I found her so utterly reviling.

She browsed the closet I shared with my roommate and remarked to the other girl, "Wow, you have so many more clothes than her!" And it wasn't the truth of the statement that bothered me or even that she'd said it — it was that she'd said it as if I weren't there when I so clearly was. I was visibly invisible. And I hated this perfectly skinny girl almost as much as I hated myself.

I had unwittingly tethered how I looked to who I was, and any failing of the former became, to me, a damning of the latter — and the opinion of men was my measuring stick. In spite of my Freshman Fifteen, boys still liked me enough to flirt that fall, but when I got engaged in the winter, I lost their attention. When I got married over spring break, I lost my freedom, and when my pregnant belly ballooned, I lost my naturally thin body — and all the worth I'd tied to it—entirely. And by the time I looked at the new mother in the mirror that summer, I had lost my real self.

My culture had told me I needed to fit in, and I could not. My society had told me I needed to stay thin, and I did not. And so I got the message: I *was* not.

Our understanding of ourselves and the worth of those selves are, in great part, products of the societies and cultures in which we live. Each woman in this section shares a story of a socially or culturally communicated message of worth. Marilyn aches seeing her Pakistani friends relegated to second-class citizenship, and she aches to see Jesus restore them as tangibly as he did for the women in the Bible. Jennifer shares the sinking experience of peer rejection and the buoying experience of peer acceptance. Deborah reels from her collision with the glass ceiling, and she picks herself back up, stronger for the fight. Alexandra learns that her Colombian home views women as beneath men, but she learns that her God sees all as equally beloved. When she goes to work with sex-trafficked women in Germany, Idelette finds that humility and love are the clearest ways to connect across different languages and socioeconomic status. Melody struggles her whole life with not fitting in, and she finds that the answer to her belonging has been sewn into her being from the start.

Though the places and situations are as varied as the individuals who have lived in them, the effect is the same. We take in messages from those outside influences as we take in food—naturally, necessarily, and with significant impact. If the food we eat is contaminated, it affects us internally and profoundly. So we must pay attention to what we're taking in, and where it's unhealthy, we have to choose not to allow it and find what we need to take in for our wellness instead.

Relentless Pursuit

Marilyn Gardner

I smelled the woman before I saw her. She was sitting on a rope bed with legs folded gracefully under her, her clothing and bed covering damp. Her lovely face told a million stories but the story that overshadowed all others was a story of defeat.

The hospital room reeked of urine, made worse by the small fan struggling to cool the ninety-degree heat. I tried not to hold my nose and willed myself to look beyond the stench. For the first time I was seeing the effects of poor prenatal care—a fistula between her bladder and vagina caused the woman to leak urine all day, every day. There was no relief. No time when she could feel clean. Not only had she lost her baby, she had been cast out from her home—no one, least of all a man, wanted to be close to someone who smelled this way.

I was in Pakistan working at a women's and children's hospital in a small city in the desert. It was an area where clean water and sanitation were not readily available and disease was common. I was no stranger to this—though I was born in America, Pakistan had been my home since I was three months old.

As a girl growing up in Pakistan I knew I was loved and valued, my place in the family portrait secure and privileged, a place of honor. The only girl in a family of four boys, I challenged the statistical geniuses who warned my mother that it was "unusual to have a girl after that many boys!" and was emotionally spoiled from my first breath. Even at the most awkward of stages, I lived in a world of princess privilege. My best friend in Pakistan was also the only girl in her family. She was dark-haired and beautiful and I imagined us both as exotic princesses. We would be swept away by handsome princes who resembled George Harrison from the Beatles.

But the world that surrounded me presented a different picture. As a child I distinctly remember sobs from a woman who had given birth to a baby girl. Her tears came from a place deep within her soul. Not giving birth to a boy put her in a precarious position in her marriage and in her future. Would she be replaced by another wife who could bring a boy into the world? Would she be relegated to a life of servant status in the home of her in-laws because she had no son to care for her as she became older? The world around me painted a picture of women as supply and demand, of women as property that could be bartered for or replaced. Just beyond the walls of my home I saw a portrait of women that had been scarred and damaged until it was no longer worth the frame that held it. This was not a world of princess privilege.

This was a world where life could be brutally unfair; a world where a teenage girl could be engaged to a much older man, third in his list of wives; a world where a newborn girl was cause for tears, not rejoicing; a world where men were of value and women, often scorned. It was at 13 that I realized had I been a Pakistani girl, my choices and path in life would be different. I thought about being married to a 40-year-old, taking the place as second wife, status and identity suspect until that first male child was born. I struggled to make sense of these two worlds—*Why me favored? Why them denied?*

But it became more than an outsider's view—it was the reality that as I grew breasts and hips and engaged in the world outside my home, I too became an object, a possession. This was reinforced through eyes that took me in from toes to head, the unsolicited touching by boys and young men, all borne silently because that's what we did.

So it wasn't just the smell of urine that made me gasp for air that day as I left the hospital room. It was those questions of favor and privilege, denial and disadvantage. Why were women objects, commodities to be used then tossed according to cultural norms? And above all, the question that crushed the air around so I cried out for oxygen was why this woman had to sit all day in her own urine, rejected by everyone but her mother and sister, mourning the death of her baby even as she was mourning the death of her life.

Where was the God of Deborah? Deborah, whose words "March on, my soul; be strong" echoed God's affirmation of the strength and leadership of women. Where was the God of Hagar? Hagar, who was cast out in a desert as hot as the one where I stood, certain she would die, only to be met by the living God and living water. Where was the God of Mary? Mary, who was greeted with the words, "The Lord is with you," words unmistakable in their promise. My soul ached with the absence of God; the woman's eyes mirrored the vacancy I felt.

And in my soul cry I was taken to another place, much like the place I was standing. It was a place with mud buildings, dusty streets, and crowds of people. A place where water and sanitation were often lacking, a place where, daily, men prayed the prayer, "God, I thank you that I was not born a woman or a dog!" I was taken back to a time when a woman was asking the same questions with a defeated spirit and vacant eyes—a woman who had been unclean, bleeding for twelve years, discarded by society. But she had an "if only" on her lips. *If only I could touch his clothes. If only I could reach out. If only...* And in that moment—that moment of touch when her fingers reached Jesus' robe, that moment of connection with the living God—she was healed. But that's not where the story ends. Jesus would not let it rest. In a world where she had been cast aside, he asked her to come to him. He was relentless. He kept looking. He kept seeking.

And despite her fear, despite everything she heard and believed about her worth she came forward. Raw fear made her tremble but his relentless pursuit won. And she heard words that were clear and strong, words that were sweet, words that told her for the first time in her life who she really was. She heard that she was a daughter, beloved by a father God. She heard that her faith, evidenced through her actions, was not in vain. She heard that she was healed. She heard that she could go in peace. She heard and she knew she was free from her suffering.

Would this God come through for the woman sitting in the hospital room? Would the relentless seeker not stop until he had been able to say, "Daughter, your faith has healed you. Go in peace and be free from your suffering"? I choked outside the hospital room. I hoped that the doctor would think it was my weak stomach responding to the smell instead of my urgent tears for this woman, urgent tears for the 13-year-old married to the 40-year-old, and urgent tears for me, all collecting in my throat.

It was as though the doctor could read my thoughts. She looked at me, eyes clear and sure: "She'll be okay. It's a simple surgery and her life will be changed." And she was right. Over the weeks that followed I saw the relentless seeker heal and change her life through the hands of gifted physicians. I saw a life changed through a simple surgery by a skilled surgeon, a long recovery in the safety of a hospital, and a relentless seeker's saying, "Daughter, your faith has healed you. Go in peace and be free from your suffering!"

There were to be other times when I would see women who sat aside, alone on their rope beds; women who were cast out and shunned, who had seen too much of life and whose faces bore the marks of their pain. And there were to be times when I would be that woman—a woman whose worth was questioned, whose value was challenged, who knew loneliness and defeat. But I would never forget this woman and this story; I would never stop believing that worth could be restored by a relentless pursuit, an unstoppable love, and the words, "Go in peace and be free from your suffering."

The Real Me

Jennifer Deibel

I stared in amazement at my reflection in the mirror. *Is that really me? Can I really be this pretty?* The baby pink turtleneck lent a soft glow to my cheeks. My just-longer-than-shoulder-length blonde hair bore a sheen unlike I'd ever seen, and every piece was in place. Never before had I felt so beautiful, and it couldn't have happened at a better time. It was the night of the sixth grade roller skating party, and what I saw in the mirror gave me just the confidence boost I needed to ask him to skate.

The hours that followed are a blur. I don't remember eating dinner, getting in the car, or arriving at the rink. I don't even remember the time spent skating, waiting for a slow song to be played. But I remember that when the perfect song came through the speakers, I sent my best friend over to ask him, as is the custom in pre-pubescent "mating rituals."

I waited nervously for her to return with his answer. *Would he skate with me? Did he like me? Was I worth it?* The answer she delivered socked me in the gut, stealing every last ounce of breath from my lungs:

"Why would I want to have anything to do with a dog like her?"

I tried to play it cool as I shrugged with what I hoped came off as nonchalance and murmured under my breath, "Oh well, who cares." But once in the safe confines of a filthy bathroom stall, I collapsed in a heap, bawling in silence. *This year was supposed to be different. I was supposed to matter.* His reaction to a simple invitation to skate in an oval for two-and-a-half minutes was the falling of a small pebble onto an already precarious mountainside, initiating an avalanche I couldn't hope to outrun: I had been treated with such disdain, by guy and girl alike, since moving to the area two years prior.

I grew up in a loving home being valued, cherished, supported. But deep inside, I never believed it. Any of it. When I was told and shown that I was beautiful and valuable, something echoed in the core of my being, *It's a lie.* I believed they said things merely because that's what a father, mother, or teacher is supposed to say. And when they told me God wanted me, cherished me, saw me as beautiful, I believed that it, too, was a lie — true for everyone else, just not for me.

What value I disbelieved from God, I looked for among my peers — cute boys and cool girls. I turned myself inside out, desperate for some nod of approval from those that I thought mattered. I wore things I didn't like. I listened to music I didn't understand. I left the favorite things about myself at home, hidden, stuffed inside the dusty drawer of my heart, buried under slouch socks and New Kids On The Block lyric sheets. I lived in a daily hell I had plummeted into by ripping out the threads that God had painstakingly woven into my being, all in a desperate attempt to be anyone but who I was.

I kept thinking if I could just get it right, wear the right things, look like *her* — or even *her*, just not me — then suddenly they would see, and show me, what I was worth. Instead, daily ridicule slowly grated the flesh of my heart like lemon zest, until finally all that was left was the bitter, stringy, ugly part that everyone throws away. They discarded me simply because I didn't wear an inverted triangle on my butt cheek or a blue rectangle on the heel of impossibly flat canvas shoes.

What started as torment gave way to all-consuming fear as the popular girls made daily threats "to kick my ass." Terror gripped me every time I was forced to set foot outside the classroom. Thank God I never had to walk home, or I'm sure I would have been pummeled on countless occasions. But really, my heart would have preferred the physical bruises of a fist fight, which heal quickly, as opposed to the life-long emotional turmoil that accompanies such verbal and mental abuse.

The voices of my peers drowned out those of the people who truly mattered. The more family and true friends spoke of goodness, mercy, and value to me, the louder the screaming in my soul shrieked the opposite. We moved to a new city and I entered high school with a vile mix of desperation and hope—desperate to do whatever it took to finally matter, and the faint hope that things would be different this time, that I would be different. My heart, I feared, would not recover from continued rejection as a human being, and hope dangled in front of me, propelling me forward. However, my spirit was weary with warring and effort. My soul was frantically pushing and fighting against the current of grace, deaf to the hope and identity offered in the strong, tender embrace of God. I had abandoned who I was made to be in an effort to become who "they" wanted me to be and earn the approval of the very ones who brought so much pain and devastation to my life. With the fresh start of a new school on the horizon, determination outweighed exhaustion as I made a vow in the silent recesses of my mind to be myself this time, whoever that was.

If you had asked me at the time if I believed miracles still occurred, I would have said yes. If you had asked me if a miracle had ever occurred in my own life, I would have said, "Apart from being saved from hell, fire, and damnation… no." (Because that's what you're supposed to say, you know—that it's a miracle you're here and saved—even though you're miserable and still living like a slave to the lies sown deep in your heart. *That's what good Christian girls do.*) But a miracle did happen in my own life, and not until I saw it in hindsight did I recognize it.

In this new city, new school, God surrounded me with a group of friends that truly valued me. The real me. I was loved and celebrated and nurtured like I had never been before by a group of people my own age. Slowly, I began to heal. Some of the lies began to fade, or at least I came to recognize them as such when they shouted in the depths of my soul. All of the good and love and worth that my parents, brother, and small handful of friends sowed into me over the years finally began to germinate in my spirit.

I wish I could say that now I know my full value in Christ, that it's tangible and real. I wish I could say that. But the truth is there are still dark days. Days when his voice haunts me—*a dog like her*—days when their jeers and threats surface and my spirit believes the lies. But the light in the darkness is that it is not every day. There are days now when I know who I am in God, when my worth to Him and my circle of influence on this planet is clear and vivid in my heart—and my spirit believes the truth.

Patchwork Umbrellas

Deborah Bryan

Winter rain was slowly washing away my spirit, yet it was only late December. I knew many more months of Eugene, Oregon's incessant rain awaited me, a thought I could barely handle.

I wasn't at all confident I could handle the reality. Moving was imperative. I just wasn't certain where I should move until a conversation with my sister's favorite hair stylist illuminated the answer for me: I needed to return to Los Angeles, where I'd studied law until 2004.

The sunshine beckoned. Job offers did not. Undeterred, I quit my job and moved into a girlfriend's Monterrey Park guest room, with the blessing of her husband.

After a first glacial week of job hunting, I received a number of recruitment phone calls the same afternoon. Several of the jobs were appealing, but only one was exactly what I'd hoped to find. I whooped and hollered when the job was offered to me a few weeks later. I'd done it—I'd really done it! Following my heart had paid off!

My first couple of days on the job were delightful. I was doing what I'd been trained to do in my previous job, but without the daunting hours or responsibilities. I was, remarkably, being paid more to do less.

But by the end of my first full week, I wasn't feeling so elated. Things weren't going at all as I'd expected. I couldn't put my finger on what was wrong, but I was disturbed by how my manager treated me more like his secretary than a contract negotiator. His need for photocopies or note-taking—often communicated via shouts from his office—seemed to supersede my need to complete document revisions for even the most urgent acquisitions.

After several such incidents, I talked myself up to saying no. It was a frightening prospect since I had a truckload of debt and a newly signed lease that required the ongoing income of a not-fired employee, but I was finding it increasingly difficult to complete complex tasks with his frequent interruptions.

When I finally told my manager that I'd get to one of his tasks as soon as I completed the one at hand, he stepped into my cube and hovered over me. "What is it you're doing that's so important you can't do what I told you to?" he demanded. "Show me. Now." I showed him the document I was revising and explained the reason timing was important. I don't remember whether he agreed with my assessment, but I do remember his angry scowl. I remember how, incensed to have his authority questioned, he began finding his way into my cube to hover over my shoulder with ever-increasing frequency. Each day, I dreaded the morning a little more. I feared I'd escaped the oppressive gloom of one downpour only to land myself in another.

A few short weeks after starting a job I'd believed would be perfect, I was fervently hunting another job. Positions requiring software contract negotiators with a meager one to two years of experience were few and far between. My despair grew.

One day, I decided I would rather lose my job than permit it to continue along its course. I set up time to talk with my manager. Sitting in his office, I explained to him that I needed blocks of time uninterrupted to complete the more time-intensive tasks of my job. I let him know in clear but calm language that I wasn't comfortable with his physically entering my small, semi-enclosed cube, but that I welcomed phone calls, emails and even short, recurring meetings to discuss which tasks were in the works and which were in store.

He told me he hadn't understood how "formal" I was, but that he'd try to meet my "special needs." I was already exhausted from the exchange and the weeks of experiences leading up to it, so I bit my tongue and accepted that as the best possible outcome in the circumstances. Work was better for a day or two, but the rain returned harsher and louder than ever when old patterns emerged quickly, and worse. When I pointed this out to my manager, he replied that he was, in fact, my manager, not vice versa.

Outside, the skies were blue, but I could barely see them. I wished I'd stayed in Eugene, where the literal rain was, at least, easy to escape. This metaphorical torrent felt inescapable.

I felt ashamed constantly. I wondered what was wrong with me, that my manager felt enabled to treat me as his servant instead of a valued negotiator. I saw the camaraderie he had with the male negotiator on our three-negotiator team and thought, *It's because I'm a woman. He feels he has power over me because I'm a woman.*

This conclusion was supported by a couple of facts. First, the other woman negotiator on our team faced similar difficulties. Second, I learned that the negotiator I had replaced was a woman who had asked too many questions before being fired for insubordination. Understanding these things didn't make me feel any less deflated by the experience, but I was comforted as much as dismayed that it wasn't just me subject to my manager's bad behavior.

Together, my female colleague and I decided to approach the company's human resources department to file a complaint. We hoped that our doing so might lead our manager to remember that broadly couched corporate policies about harassment applied to all employees — managers included.

Our human resources representative listened somewhat attentively but presented her shocking conclusion in a few memorable words. "Dumb down or quit," she said, before proceeding to tell us that we had no idea what it was like to endure real on-the-job hardship. As an older black woman, she assured us, she'd had to endure much, much worse. Even worse than our manager's treating us disparagingly was being told we were bringing it upon ourselves by trying to be too smart.

Human Resources conducted an official review, which culminated in the none-too-surprising determination that our manager was not discriminating against us on the basis of our gender, nor in any notable way at all that they could discern.

Pitterpatterpitterpatterpitterpatter. The rain kept falling, but I had no umbrella to keep it off my head.

I continued documenting my ongoing concerns in emails to Human Resources. I let them know I would be filing a complaint against the company since the company itself had proven uninterested in advocating for all of its employees. I hoped the threat of outside intervention would prompt them to reconsider their approach to ongoing complaints.

Nine eternal weeks after starting my "perfect" job, I landed another one. I breathed a sigh of relief when I emailed my one-week notice, only to find myself shocked anew when my manager stormed into my cube and demanded an explanation. I documented this exchange in an email to Human Resources, explaining that my manager entered my cube uninvited and hovered within one to two feet of me while demanding I tell him my reason for leaving. He didn't move even when I told him his proximity combined with his raised voice made me uncomfortable.

I pointed out the specific corporate policy this behavior violated and included its text within my email. Human Resources nevertheless derided me the rest of the afternoon via a series of increasingly absurd emails that I couldn't believe it was documenting in writing.

When I left the company at the end of the week, I was too exhausted to feel elated. If this was victory, it felt a lot like defeat, personally and professionally.

How could even my most concerted efforts have resulted in little more than mockery? What on earth could I expect in the future if this kind of behavior was condoned at a corporate level? I feared.

I'll never forget the vulnerability or sorrow of being categorically dismissed or of being told there wouldn't ever have been a problem if I had just dumbed myself down. Neither will I forget my intense fear about what might await me at my new job, a fear that took months to fade despite dozens of indicators that my coworkers and management alike respected and valued my feedback.

But days passed. The rain slowed. Little beams of sun forced their way through the clouds to dance upon my uplifted face.

More and more infrequently, with increasing calm, I thought of the downpour I'd escaped. I looked at the lightness of my new life and hoped only light sprinkles were in store for me. My hope was immense, but I even exceeded my own expectations; I vowed I would keep making my own figurative umbrellas in case future perpetrators tried to define the problem and resolution in ways that suited only them.

As I thought of umbrellas already built from a patchwork of hard experience and hope, I took comfort in remembering my resistance. I'd felt hopeless, but I hadn't let my actions be defined by that hopelessness. I'd fought. Remembering that was even more powerful than remembering the horrible reason I'd had to fight.

I'd fought because—regardless of what anyone else does or does not believe—I am worth the fight. Fortunately, despite my fears the past would perpetuate itself in my new jobs, my only "fights" since learning this have been downright mundane.

But if there ever again comes a time where they are not? I'm ready. I know the feeling of the sun on my face, and I know better now how to seek it. The rain may fall again, but I trust the umbrellas I have made and the light within my heart to sustain me until I once again walk with my face lifted toward the sun.

Blessed to Be a Woman

Alexandra Rosas

By the time I was seven years old, I could perform our Hispanic family's dinner routine with my eyes closed; I was so well trained in the details of how a meal was to be served. First, my two brothers were given their plates even though one of them was younger than I was and the other, only 18 months older. Once the boys received their dinner, then my three sisters and I were able to get our own plates—after we were sure that my brothers had everything they needed: drinks, more bread, enough silverware.

By the time I was seven years old, I was old enough to do this work automatically. I was also old enough to feel hurt by it. I have often wondered why rather than resenting this unfair cultural estimation of male over female, I instead felt bewildered by it. I just could not understand why it was me, as a girl, who was seen as the lesser sex in our home and therefore—I thought—in the world. It could have been the 117th time that I set the plated food before my brothers—who were always gracious and thankful—and yet, on the 118th time, I would still cast my eyes down, used to my role but not accepting of it, as I served them. I felt so ashamed at having to put myself beneath them and at their command. And I know I did not imagine the guilt they felt in return at having to sit quietly as they were served by the very same sister they had just played a game of Monopoly with. We each felt powerless, following blindly in a situation that we did not understand. But this was what we were taught from as young as we could remember: The men were what were important in the world, and the women were the ones that came after.

Hispanic culture has long treated women as the less valued sex. Few things make a man prouder in my culture than his wife's giving birth to a son. Women are loved and protected, but they are seen as a decoration, and their place is in the home. They are not the ones served first, nor are they the ones that cause a father's chest to burst with pride as when he hears the words, "It's a son!"

My five siblings and I were raised by my Colombian grandmother, a lovely, nurturing woman who had Jesus as the center of her every thought and action. She was a kind woman and a grand story teller. A story she told us often was about her life in South America. She herself had been the firstborn in her family. A girl—a very disappointing girl—when every family back then wished for the blessing of a son as the firstborn. As she told this story, I would wonder how her feelings could be unhurt, knowing her father and mother wished for a son instead.

In South America, to have a firstborn be a boy is extremely good fortune and a promise of a fruitful life. When my own mother found out she was pregnant with her first, she naturally prayed for a son. Every day, she would go to her small town's church and make offerings to have a boy. Her firstborn was a girl. She feared my father would leave her, and she prayed that her second pregnancy would finally be a son. Another girl was born. My father was too ashamed to go into town with the announcement. To have another girl is a poor reflection on a man's prowess. With her third pregnancy, my mother promised the Virgin Maria del Carmen that she would name the child after her if it were a boy. My brother, Gabriel del Carmen, was the third child and first son born to my parents. My father set off fireworks on the night he was born.

I would listen to these stories, feeling so sad and wondering if no one else felt the pain that I did at being told that as a girl, I was not cause for celebration. I would ask myself why a woman was worth less than a man. Who first said this? Where did it come from? Why are girls lesser than boys, and why aren't parents just as happy and proud at the birth of a daughter? I never understood since I never felt lesser than my brothers, even though that message was spoken every day in our house.

As my siblings and I grew up, a household of four girls and two boys, we would often hear my mother lament, "If only I had been blessed with more boys than girls. God didn't see it to bless me this way." This was a puzzling comment to my ears since my three sisters and I did the lion's share of the housework; cooking, laundry, dusting—anything that had to be done was done by the girls of the family. I don't remember my brothers helping in any area, something I complained about to myself. But I respected my mother too much to question why she would wish for more boys even though we girls were the ones running the household of nine people.

I could ask my grandmother, though. She had an easy, approachable way about her, and one day, as we sat together while she sewed on the buttons that had fallen off my brother's shirt, I asked, "Abuela, why does everyone love boys more than girls?" For some reason, I thought my evident unhappiness with this would anger her, but, instead, not even looking up from her sewing, she answered, "That's the way it is, my granddaughter. It's always been like this."

I would sit with my five siblings around my grandmother as she would tell stories of life in Colombia while she cooked, sewed, or folded laundry. She would say things that hurt, but it wasn't so much a matter of my wishing she wouldn't say what she did as it was hearing her resignation at her life, having been born female. I loved my grandmother deeply, and I can remember my heart breaking as well as being angered as she would tell a story, stop, and sigh, "I never had the good fortune to be born a man." These stories kept me asking myself, *What is wrong with being born female?*

I was never able to accept my culture's view of women being lesser than men even though I had heard and seen and lived the message in my home every moment of the day. It couldn't be the way that things were meant to be. When my grandmother would tell stories about Jesus and His admiration and devotion to His mother, I couldn't believe in my heart that we as females were the less desirable sex in the world. I don't mean I was thinking about the issues of women's rights or equal rights; I was thinking about the matter of being created by the hand of God, that we were nothing less than equally valued by Him. Not as in the eyes of society or among cultures, but in the eyes of God—my God—surely we were equal.

Though my grandmother lamented being born a woman and my mother cherished her sons more than her daughters, I have never wished I was born anything other than what I am: a woman. Unlike my grandmother, I have always felt blessed to be a woman, so very comfortable and natural in the sex God chose for me. I have not spent a day in my life when I have wished for anything other than who I am.

Growing up hearing my grandmother's stories, told with a firm, unshakable belief in our Lord, my siblings and I were left with an appetite to learn more about Christ, to continue to discover this Lord even more. It was this pursuit of getting to know Jesus as my own Jesus that led me to a college Bible study called, "Women of the Bible." The group's leader was a woman who could speak hours without ever consulting a note card. She would run through scripture verses, shouting out passages and never once losing her place in her talk, as the rest of us flipped through our Bibles, our hair flying in the wind from the turning of our pages.

The memory of one life-changing night's study still brings a lump to my throat. This woman began telling us the story of the resurrection of Christ in a way that has made me retell this story to anyone who will listen. We were all gathered, college students, male and female, and our instructor began, "Do you know how I know Jesus is real? Because He did something so radical, so against the culture of that time, that no man in his right mind would ever do what Jesus did… if they wanted the story of their resurrection to spread."

As we all leaned in, barely sitting on the edge of our chairs, she went on, "Jesus did what He did, He arose the way He did, because He wanted to say something to the world. His message is about salvation, and ascension, and life after death, but it is also about us. About men and women and how He is risen again for all. Do you know who Jesus first appeared to after three days in the tomb? He appeared to women. He told women to spread the message that He still lives."

She explained the earth-shattering significance of Jesus' decision to first be seen by women at the most important part of His existence on earth. She told us, "Back then, in Jesus' time, no one listened to women. Women were property, second-class citizens, thought of as little more than children, prone to hysteria and overcome with emotions. What a woman had to say, no man cared to hear or would take seriously. Yet Jesus chose women to see Him first and spread His message. Why? Because we are essential to His story; we are that important. We can be counted on to do what it takes when something needs to be done. This is Jesus saying, 'you are important and necessary to my world.'"

As I heard her words, my eyes filled with tears and my heart, with longing. All I wanted at that moment was for my grandmother to still be alive to hear about how we were deliberately chosen by God to see His Son first. That we are so important that we were placed at the tomb that third morning. I wanted her here so I could run home and tell her this. This: That God believes in us so much that He chose us, that he needs us, that His world demands the presence of a woman in it.

How I wished that night that my grandmother were still here, so I could joyfully celebrate with her and shout the news that though man told her that her place was below him, our God tells us otherwise. We are equal in His eyes, not one over the other. I would search for her time-worn Bible, turn to Genesis 1:27, and through eyes blurry with tears, I would turn to her and show her, "Right here, Abuela. See? It says, 'In His Image. He created them, male and female.'"

Brokenness: Our Perfect Equal Sign

Idelette McVicker

I asked the kids to help me haul six plastic zipper bags full of pennies from our car to the church sanctuary. I'd received a last-minute invitation to add my voice to the line-up at our annual women's conference. I wasn't on the roster, but it didn't matter — wasn't God precisely speaking to me about worth, about how God can take my nothingness and turn it into something good, even a miracle?

I had ten minutes and I wanted each woman to go away with something tangible, a reminder of her worth. I didn't have time to bake bread for the hundreds of women, but as I prayed, "Lord, what can I give them?" I remembered the bags full of pennies in our storage closet in the basement.

If Jesus could lift up a little boy's picnic lunch to heaven, give thanks, and feed a whole crowd with that miracle, God could use pennies to speak worth. What I wanted more than anything was for every woman in that room to understand that our lives and our efforts, our broken dreams and our broken stories could become exactly the meal Jesus chooses to use on a sunny day at a picnic on a hill.

He could also use my scraps, my leftovers, my brokenness, my not-enough-ness on a rainy day on the streets of Berlin.

It was the day I met Danika.[4]

---

4   Name has been changed.

My friend Emma and I were walking along a back street of the city, inviting any women who let us talk to them to a small ministry center for prostitutes and drug addicts called Café Neustart, meaning "new beginnings." We were part of a group of eight North American women journeying through southern and central Europe to learn about the source and demand sides of sex trafficking. On that Thursday, we partnered with a ministry called Alabaster Jar to host a lunch for the women on the street.

Danika and her friend stood inside the traffic, selling to the highest bidder—or the way it looked on that gray, rainy day, any bidder at all. We had heard rumours of some girls on the street lowering the price of a blowjob so much, now others couldn't survive.

We watched a different kind of worth, an economic worth, measured in minutes, appearance, and performance and translated into German Marks play out in front of our eyes.

When Emma and I first approached the two Czech women, the four of us huddled together under a black umbrella, seeking cover from the August showers. We showed them the invitation in their native Czech. They were simple invitations copied and printed in Bulgarian, Hungarian, Czech, Russian and Slovak—some of the languages of the women who frequented this side of Berlin.

Neither of them spoke much German, only enough to get by on the streets.

Enough of a language to flirt a little. Enough of a language to buy milk and bread. Enough of a language to bum a cigarette. Enough of a language to tell a john how much.

Emma and I were sent out into the rain that day because I was the only one in our group who could speak some German. I remember accepting the assignment with some hesitation: the outside loomed cold and unfamiliar; inside the café was comfortable and friendly. But the moment we stepped over the threshold and into the street, I also stepped outside of myself. I knew it was an honour to serve God's daughters on the streets.

As my tongue curled around the foreign consonants, looking for the teenage memories of embedding this language into my brain, five years of high school German finally felt like they had a greater purpose. Speaking the sentences—such a simple invitation to come and have something to eat and drink, get a haircut or your nails painted—my fumbled grammar felt loaded with meaning.

I was in a place of complete humility, keenly aware that my German couldn't achieve much more than to order a meal or find a train station. As I reflected on my feelings of lack, however, I realized my less-than-perfect, almost-forgotten German was the ideal meeting ground for these women's German ability. Our broken sentences were the perfect equal sign.

While we talked to Danika and her friend, they looked eager to join us. We pointed to Café Neustart down the street and they nodded enthusiastically. We said goodbye and let them work while we walked around the block and talked to more women along the strip. Then, on our way back, I caught a glimpse of Danika's face: pained, vacant, lost. It was as if she had just seen or experienced the most horrific thing. The words "bad date" rang like a siren through my head.

My heart sank and I murmured inwardly, *I guess there's no chance of them coming to the café now.* My own hopes of their experiencing some dignity, love, worth—not anyone asking anything of them in return—felt shattered. Danika wouldn't even look at us, so I had to let her go. Still, we walked and prayed.

About an hour later, the two women walked through the door at Café Neustart. Danika kept to the margins of the room and wouldn't even accept a cup of coffee. She watched for a very long time, while her friend, the more gregarious one, started talking to everyone and even sat down for a haircut. Then the two friends moved to the bead table and started stringing elaborate necklaces. They sat there for a long time, while other women came, ate, got haircuts, talked, drank more coffee, had their nails painted, talked some more, and left.

The café was abuzz with conversation and connection. I hoped and prayed: *Lord, show yourself to Danika. Show her something different. Show her that people care.*

As the afternoon progressed, her posture relaxed. She got up, took a plate and finally helped herself to the rye bread, cold meats, homemade potato salad, and fresh watermelon chunks. I eased into the idea that she wasn't going to run out the door any time soon. And she didn't. She was one of the last ones to get a haircut that afternoon. She was one of the last ones to leave.

I watched her sit back and slowly soak in the pleasure of being fussed over. Her eyes opened up and smiled with every snip as our stylist friend brought transformation. We oohed and ahhed and took lots of pictures.

When we said goodbye—almost wordless—I held her tightly and squeezed as much love as I possibly could into her skin, hoping it would go straight to her heart. I wanted her to remember that afternoon in a little café in Berlin when Heaven came down and whispered, "You are beautiful, you are worthy, you are loved."

God hadn't required a perfect offering, but only my willingness to bring what I had.

The Secret of a Woman

Melody J. Wachsmuth

My mom turned the car into the parking lot, and I sat in my seat, excited and nervous for a new season of soccer. My three brothers and I had been playing over the summer—I knew I was strong and fast. I loved sports, but I also loved curling up with a good book, writing poetry and stories, and drinking tea in dainty china cups.

I walked up to my new team and realized there were no familiar faces from last year. Since most of the girls attended the local junior high together while I went to a private school, I usually began as an outsider. I wasn't worried—making friends was never hard for me. This year, I noticed some of the girls wore makeup, and as I stared at their lips, glossy with a pink color, I thought that it was strange to put on lipstick for soccer practice. The coach had us introduce ourselves to each other and then we began some drills.

"How was practice?" my mom asked as I plopped into the car afterwards.

"Fine. I like the coach. He looks like the Pillsbury Dough Boy and can even imitate the giggle!"

My mom smiled. "Good. I'm sure you'll make friends in no time."

***

"Oh, Melody, you have such beautiful hair and skin. If I could just make you up, you would look so pretty!"

I forced a laugh and a smile, hiding the flash of shame and anger twisted together in an ugly and familiar partnership.

"Oh, I don't think so," I said, pretending to study and touch up my face in the mirror.

"Please?" she said. "It would be so much fun."

I turned and started walking out of my college dorm bathroom.

"Maybe later," I hedged. "I have class."

***

I turned away from my teammates' scorn, trying to appear nonchalant, when I felt a hand sweep across my back.

"Oh my gosh, she's not wearing a bra. Melody doesn't wear a bra!"

Shame, the unwelcome guest, wrapped its smothering tendrils around me, and I urgently wished to disappear. My other teammates stared at me, curious and mute in a shared adolescent conspiracy.

"I have a bra," I lied. "I'm just not wearing it today."

Amber* shared a glance with her sidekick, Jennie*, and they both stared at me with disgusted derision.

"Yeah right," Jennie said. "Why wouldn't you wear it to practice?" They laughed and walked to where the rest of the team was forming lines. I slunk to the back of the line, keeping space between me and the last girl, pretending to be deep in thought as I stared at the grass.

In truth, my parents had been trying to get me to wear a bra for months, but I remained in denial about the strange metamorphosis of my body. Athletic and tough, I had no problem keeping up with my brothers. A bra would only slow me down, I thought, and at the very least it acknowledged that I was different from them—a difference that seemed to imply weakness.

Later, I snuck into my parents' bedroom and rifled through my mother's lingerie drawer. I pulled out a bra and went into their bathroom to try it on.

"Melody? What are you doing in there?" My mom knocked on the door. It wasn't long until the door opened and I confessed the latest incident involving my tormenters. My mom promised that she would take me to go find an appropriately sized bra—a promise triggering conflicting sensations of both dread and relief.

***

I stepped into the reception hall, admiring the beautiful decorations and the tables laden with food.

"Melody!" A friend came up and squeezed my arm. "You look so beautiful! Come get a drink!"

I looked at her dress, stylish and perfect, fitting over her slim figure. Her hair fell smooth and gleaming onto her shoulders. As usual, her makeup was exquisitely done, her eyes standing out beautifully from her flawless skin. Suddenly, my earlier feeling of glamour vanished, leaving behind a sense of awkward clumsiness. I had tried to blow dry my hair in an effort to get rid of the frizz, but now I could feel it like a halo around my head. I caught a glimpse of my face in the mirror by the doorway, and my makeup looked childish and sloppy. Envy and jealously consumed my earlier excitement and I wondered what it would feel like to know what she knew — what it would feel like to know how to be a woman.

"You look beautiful too," I said smiling, my face like a concrete wall guarding my shame. "Let's go get a drink."

***

Amber's eyes traveled down my body, a search beam looking for any flaw. "Oh my gosh. Your legs are so hairy! Jennie, she doesn't shave her legs!"

In dawning horror, I realized that my legs were indeed much hairier than the other girls'. My legs were strong — they could climb trees and rope swings, run faster than anybody in my class, jump to shoot a basketball. But I had never noticed that they were hairy.

I slumped in the car, feeling relief as my mom drove away from the school. "What happened today?" my mom asked.

"Can I shave my legs?" I replied. My mom sighed.

"Of course — I'll show you how." She looked at me. "You can quit, you know."

I felt something stubborn rise up in me. *I will not quit*, I thought to myself.

"No, I'll finish out the season." But after that, I'm never playing soccer again.

***

I left the dress store, satisfied with my successful shopping expedition. I had found a dress I thought was beautiful and planned to wear it to my cousin's wedding. Turquoise was my favorite color, and the dress was a unique, earthy print of turquoise and brown. Now in my thirties, I had become aware that I was a fashion chameleon, dressing to blend in so that no one would be able to see my under layers of confusion and insecurity. *Even if I knew what I liked, would I have the courage to express it if it were different from everyone else?* I thought this turquoise dress was a step in the right direction.

I showed it to my mom and she donned her polite face. "You don't think you'll be cold in that?"

"No, I'll wear a shawl over it," I said.

Later, I was reading by the fire when she entered the room. "You know, Melody, your sister-in-law and I were talking about your dress—we don't want you to feel out of place wearing it at the wedding. I don't know that it is entirely appropriate for a winter wedding. I think most women will be wearing black dresses. Maybe you can borrow something of mine or of hers."

I stared at her in disbelief. My mother's well-meaning comment triggered twenty years of secret inner turmoil—welling up in a volcanic surge, the rage burst out in an ugly and uncontrollable confrontation:

What is so wrong with me that everyone always feels compelled to fix me?

***

I had not seen Amber for about six years when I ran into her unexpectedly one day. Shocked, I realized she did not recognize me as I walked by her. I pretended to be looking for something in my bag as I stopped unobtrusively a few paces away and studied her out of the corner of my eye. She was smaller than I remembered; the expression behind the glasses she now wore was benign and mild. Her presence projected a sense of vulnerability and I felt the giant image of her in my imagination begin to slowly deflate. I was baffled: *How could that be her?*

***

I had avoided women's conferences all my life, paranoid about being trapped in a weekend of self-disparaging insecurity, once more on the outside of women who got it. But now I lived in a different country, and, hungry for connection and interactions in my own language, I decided to attend one, albeit with much trepidation.

The speaker shared about inner freedom through forgiveness, and on the first day of the conference, images of Amber's and Jennie's contempt popped into my mind. *Are you serious?* I thought to myself. *I'm 36 years old and thinking about an incident that happened over twenty years ago?*

I tried to push the images out of my mind, but their potent presence hovered around my thoughts throughout the weekend. The last day, the speaker led us through a time of prayer to see if we needed to forgive anyone. With a sigh, I acknowledged that maybe I had never consciously and formally forgiven those girls—girls who, as my age and distance from the situation allowed me to realize, were probably very insecure themselves. I followed the speaker's directive to ask God what he thought of all those painful incidents.

Although I tried to focus and stay open-minded, I was skeptical. I was in a public hall surrounded by 60 women, and I thought such things were better dealt with privately. I waited in silence and then internally gasped when a verse entered my mind: "You formed my inward parts; you wove me in my mother's womb. My frame was not hidden from you, when I was made in secret, and skillfully wrought in the depths of the earth."[5]

I was skillfully made in secret—the truth washed over me. Perhaps this was the true mystery of womanhood all along: The God of all creativity has not fashioned a secret women's club that must be entered through certain rites of passage. Rather, I can grow into the knowledge of who God created me to be—my distinctive female personhood bears the secret of my unique formation, and God is delighted when I allow my true identity to be manifest in all aspects of my life.

***

---

5   Psalm 139:13,15

"What do I want to wear today?" I thought placidly, staring at my closet. My old anxiety-ridden thoughts knocked on my mind's door, demanding control once again: *What is everyone else going to be wearing? What if you stick out? Better to just blend in.*

But the memory of the Spirit's revealed truth surfaced once again. "I praise you, for I am fearfully and wonderfully made. Wonderful are your works, that I know very well."[6] Praising God for my uniqueness transforms fear and shame into freedom—and with this truth in my heart, I asked myself once more,

What do I want to wear today?

*Names have been changed.

Psalm 139:14

Part 4: Am I Good Enough?

Stories of Expectations and Pressures

Introduction

Tamára Lunardo

Homemaker

You like to think
I do well as a homemaker
Considering
It's not what I'm made for.

I am simply not one of the useful ones:
My seams are clumsy.
I have no gift
For creating new meals.
I cannot make tidy.

But
If home is where the heart beats strongest,
Mine is painted with smooth keystrokes.

I am not one of the simply useful ones:
My seams are graceful,
Used to bind words.
I have a gift
For creating new laughter.
I can make tidy expression
Of messy truth.

I do well as a homemaker

Considering
It's what I'm made for.
I like to think.

***

I was nineteen in a wedding dress. It almost felt like playing dress-up except that the growing belly beneath the ivory dress' empire waist was obviously entirely real. When I'd tried it on in the shop, my mom had reminded me, "You need room to accommodate your little fellow." Now I was about to walk into the sanctuary of my parents' church and make a promise even bigger than my burgeoning belly. After three months of scrambling to assemble plans, my mom said for the first time ever on that last night before my wedding, "You know, you don't have to get married."

But I didn't know because it wasn't true.

I did have to get married because I could not fail the innocent baby who would be my new son, and I could not let down the sweet boy who would be my new husband, and I could not shame the upstanding girl who would be my new self. Or at least I could not shame her any more than the bang-up job I'd already done.

As a teenager, I earned my parents' fury for having boys hiding in my room, and I earned their distrust for staying out late at parties. I was a bad girl, but I was a great achiever. So I earned excellent grades in school, superior marks at vocal competitions, a state title in speech and debate, and leading roles in school plays. I found ways to earn my parents' pride, and my own. Whatever I did, I did extremely well, and if I thought I could not do something extremely well, I would not do it at all.

And the night that I told my parents about my pregnancy—the night I saw my mom's face contort in devastated tears, the night she made me call and tell my Grammie what I'd done—I knew that I'd made an egregious wrong, and I knew that I would do the best job possible of fixing it. I would do the best job possible of fixing myself. I would have my pride again, and they would be proud again.

So I stood there, nineteen in a wedding dress—let God and family witness— and I looked into my love's big hazel eyes. I made a promise I wasn't sure was right because I was sure it was the right thing to do.

When our son was born, my young husband and I arranged our college schedules so we could trade off caring for him and attending class. I took full loads and difficult electives, I learned to cook real meals and to iron my husband's dress shirts, I earned my degree on time and with honors, and I got pregnant again to keep our kids close in age. I would not do anything but the best at the triple job of matrimony and motherhood and matriculation. I would not give anything less than my whole self.

So when a New Testament course I'd taken renewed my interest in the God I'd always believed in but hadn't thought much about, I began to visit churches and invest myself in becoming a Christian (but *really* this time). I found a place where the preaching was the spiritually deepest and the most theologically thorough I'd ever heard. The people were kind and well mannered, educated and well dressed — and I became a fast and earnest student of it all.

I learned everything I could from church — God was a Holy Father, and I was a wretched sinner, and I could not earn what Jesus had freely given, but I had really ought to act as though I'd made it worth his while. When the pastor-professor of the New Testament class found out my husband was not a Christian, he cautioned me that the weight of my husband's salvation was on my slight shoulders: "You know you can never divorce him unless he asks you to." And I learned that to obey this Father Almighty, I had to be a certain kind of wife.

I was a stay-at-home mom because I thought that was the best thing for my small children, and it would only be a little while until I could begin the fulfilling career I'd worked so hard for. I had always desperately missed my mom when she worked while I had to have dinner with just my little brother and the dad who loved him but hated me. I thought I was a stay-at-home mom because it was the very best thing I could be, but when I heard a leader in our women's Bible study say with full sincerity, "I think we all stay at home because we have the same morals," I learned the real reason. I learned that to please this Heavenly Father, I had to be a certain kind of mother.

I learned how the church people talked and how they voted and how they dressed, and I learned that to have Christ, I had to be a certain kind of Christian.

And I really wanted a Father who would accept me, so I would do my damndest to make "me" into someone acceptable. I would become the right kind of wife, and I would silently suffer emotional disconnection from the man I loved. I would become the right kind of mother, and I would turn into a zombie with decaying dreams. I would become the right kind of Christian, and I would follow practices that suffocated my heart. Then maybe I would become the right kind of person. Maybe I would finally be right.

People-pleasing takes all forms, but at its core, it is about forming ourselves into an image that we think will gain the approval of others. The hope, of course, is that if we have others' approval, then perhaps we really are okay. But people-pleasing always ultimately fails us because too much—our estimation of our worth, our very selves—is riding on the whim of fallible humans.

The women in this section share how a range of external and internal expectations and pressures caused them to form themselves into people they thought they were supposed to be at the cost of their true selves. Renée recalls how life drained from her as she struggled to be the type of mother she thought she needed to be, and how life filled her again as she returned to who she was created to be. Stephanie explores her resistance to religious and cultural ideals regarding the role of a wife, and she finds a new model of strength and love to emulate instead. Amy pulls back the mask of perfectionism to reveal not only the damage it does in smothering a person, but also the joy found in discarding that mask. Lindsay details a dangerous path from abusive spiritual pressures to the formation of an eating disorder, and she offers hope of recovery for body, mind, and soul. Kara shows how sexual harassment and the pressure to keep it quiet silence the spirit, and she finds hope to sing once more. Sarah reveals the lie of body image and offers the beauty of truth in its place.

It can be difficult to let go of the pressures and expectations we and others have placed on us because doing so leaves us open to rejection. But as we see through each of these stories, when we let go a little our steely grip on our expectations and pressures, we finally have hands open to accept the gift of who we really are.

Work Makes Whole and Holy

Renée Schuls-Jacobson

When I started my stint as stay-at-home mama, the expectation was that I was supposed to love it. Everyone told me staying at home full-time was a luxury and that I was lucky to be able to afford to do it. And I should have loved it.

I meant to.

And there were parts I did love. I loved putting my son down on a soft, flannel blanket and playing Fleetwood Mac songs, watching him kick his legs, seemingly to the beat. I loved watching him eat. By seven months, he had developed outstanding fine-motor skills, and I marveled at the way he would track one green pea, corner it, pinch it between his thumb and forefinger, and bring it easily to his mouth— never once dropping it. I loved his giggles when I would make raspberries on his belly. I loved that he learned things quickly and was easily disciplined. There were a hundred more little happinesses, but the joys were too few and too fleeting.

When we learned we would only have one child, my husband and I had one quick discussion during which we decided it would be best if I stayed at home full-time. I had gone to school, earned my master's degree, done my student teaching, and, with seven years in the classroom under my belt, I figured I could always go back.

"You're making the biggest mistake of your life," the department chair sneered when I told her I wouldn't be returning after my maternity leave expired.

And I did miss teaching. Not so much the meetings or the calls to the parents, but I missed the kids. And I missed waking up feeling like I had a larger purpose than washing the laundry or the dishes, which would only get dirty and need to be washed again.

Outwardly, I smiled and was well put-together, but privately, I felt akin to a glass of water only half-full.

I spent a lot of energy trying to make our 1973 fixer-upper feel like home. I was forever rearranging the furniture, organizing and re-organizing the spices in the pantry, changing around the knick-knacks, trying to make our outdated kitchen look more appealing, and slowly peeling dated foil wallpaper off the bathroom walls.

While my son took his daily power nap, I removed old wallpaper. I poured myself into that project; yet after the walls were washed clean, after the room was painted a perfect shade, my sense of loss stirred up, like flames out of embers.

My brain, which, at one time, effortlessly moved in a thousand million perfectly synchronized synapses, was suddenly useless, filled with noisy silence. Where once my husband and I had been equals, we now had a sharp division of labor. He was the breadwinner, out in the working world— and I was the keeper of home and hearth. *Motherhood has destroyed me,* I thought to myself, remembering a wool sweater I'd once thrown in the dryer that came out one-third its original size.

Everyone said, "Of course you feel this way. The baby is little. It will get better."

Except it didn't.

From the moment I gave birth, I was irritable and agitated and unable to rest. I laid in the darkness and waited for my son to cry. Waited for him to need me.

Even after he began sleeping through the night, I could never get back into the groove of the sleep thing. Sleep, which had always come naturally for me, was now an elusive gift that was always just out of reach.

At the end of each day, my husband and I climbed into our bed exhausted. And while he quickly fell asleep, my mind would not slow down. Though my body craved rest, my brain whirred to life, making elaborate lists that I ran through incessantly, obsessively, unable to shut it off.

Initially, I thought the anxiety was due to the newborn— but the night-waking, the insomnia, the list-making and racing thoughts continued for years, well beyond nursing and potty-training. I slept less and became more volatile.

By day, I was a bundle of activity— cooking, cleaning, and worrying over my son and other people's children. And all the while, internally, imperceptibly, my mind was shrieking and filled with quiet noise. At night, I lay awake, listening to my husband breathe— calm and even— and I was filled with despair.

A terrible sadness that would not go away.

Finally, a wise friend gave me the validation I needed to find and use a regular babysitter. Once, when my sitter came, I didn't have anywhere to go. Out of sheer boredom and needing a destination, I drove to the local airport. Before September 11, 2001, a person could go right up to any concourse and plant herself in a chair. And that is exactly what I did.

In an airport, time is important. People have places they need to be. But just sitting there— having no destination at all and knowing that all my foreseeable days were filled with the same horrible stay-at-home-mommy drudgery—I felt miserable. Contrary to the long line of screens silently announcing exotic alphabetical arrivals and departures, I felt trapped. So, I just sat there and watched everything.

I watched three blonde-haired littluns wearing matching khaki shorts and white t-shirts as they pushed their way past legs and duffel bags and backpacks and busted out, all ankles and elbows and knees, to be greeted by their grandparents who gurgled with joy as they squatted on the carpet, arms outstretched.

On that day, I took it all in and felt very little. I watched the great masses that exited alone, arrived ungreeted. I watched children following their parents, eyes down, focused on some scintillating video game, thumbs flicking, on autopilot.

Autopilot.

I knew something wasn't right. I used to be the carefree, fun girl. I used to find joy all around me. *When did I start moving on autopilot?*

I wondered. And then I caught myself in a question I did not want to answer: *If a person has all the time in the world and nothing to do, is time really a blessing?*

I went home that afternoon and thought about that question. I thought about how everyone assumed I *needed* to stay home, that I would somehow be a "bad person" if I chose a different route. I thought about the pressure I had put on myself. About how my education had taught me I needed to be super-woman, that I could and should be able to do it all. But I was terrified of doing it wrong. Terrified of disappointing everyone. Terrified of ruining my son. I spent so much energy worrying about what he was wearing and what the house looked like that I had little energy left to live. I needed to find my purpose again.

Every once in a while, I heard a small voice. Like the elephant from *Horton Hears a Who!*, a book I read to my son as he grew older, I found myself believing in a little voice that I was unable to explain to others, but I simply trusted the thing I felt to be true. By becoming mindful of that voice, I was able to consider the last time I had felt filled with true spirit.

And I knew.

When I was a high school teacher, I woke each morning before my alarm clock, filled with a sense of joy. My students energized me, and I found them endlessly fascinating. I loved to help them untangle their thoughts and watch them organize their ideas into essays.

I remembered how one day, I asked my students to write for fifteen minutes, during which time I watched them, carefully studying the way they entered into this activity. For some it was like getting into an icy pool. They put in their tiniest toe first, tentatively. Picked up their pens. Looked around. Put their pens down. Wrote a word or two. A phrase. Put the pen down. For others, writing was like taking a shower, a regular part of their daily routine. For still others, writing was like bathing in a grand, footed porcelain tub, complete with candles and bubbles and champagne.

I remembered how one girl stroked her chin with her silver-ringed thumb, her eyes dark and far-away, searching for the right words. Another held her pen point up in a closed fist, like some miniature lightning rod, waiting for inspiration to spark her hand into action.

Across the room, a student sprawled across her desk, her fiery red hair draped over her left arm. One boy made the process look easy: He slouched, carefree, clenching a blue pen in a tense left-handed grip that marked his intensity.

A lawn mower passed the window and their concentration was momentarily clipped, like the long green blades outside. They all looked up; some of them caught each other's eyes, returned to their pages. I adored them all. The way one crossed her ankles, the way that another moved her hands and furrowed her brow; the way a tall boy stretched his legs in front of him in an effort to sit comfortably behind such a dinky desk, a desk which was obviously not designed for a person of his size. It struck me that day that he was becoming a man, that his mind— indeed, all their minds—were expanding every day in my classroom. I felt the enormity of that responsibility.

I am not one to toot my own horn. There are dozens of things I cannot do: I cannot play racket sports; I cannot hook up or fix anything electronic; I can't build structures out of toothpicks the way my son does; I can't cure people's bodies. For all I can't do, there is one thing that I can: I can teach English like nobody's business.

When I told my husband that doing the stay-at-home thing was killing me, he looked positively perplexed. He said he'd die to have the chance to stay at home with our son.

But when I explained it to him—how I had felt like the Queen of Nothingness, alone in our house on the hill; how I loved our son madly, but I needed to turn my eyes *outward*, to look at people and things outside our family because there were matters that spoke to me—I thought about my place in the world in a way that I hadn't before.

I spoke with my rabbi and asked if my desire to work outside the home was selfish, and he assured me it was not. He reassured me it was possible to connect with G-d in the most secular of places, away from centers of institutionalized religion, through everyday activities that help repair the world. And he encouraged me to follow my joy because, he said, if I was spiritually full, I would inevitably convey that to my child.

After my son was born, I took a seven-year hiatus from teaching, and that was a mistake.

But I figured it out. I'm back in the classroom working as an adjunct at my local community college. And everyone is okay.

Better than okay.

I am blessed to have found a place within myself where I am at peace, where I can better balance my teaching responsibilities with the responsibilities as a parent and wife. Being in the classroom, I feel it again, that sense of greater purpose: I am on earth to help people read and write, to help them make the connection between the world on the page and the world in which they live.

Sometimes my classroom is a temple; sometimes work can be holy.

Mary, Muscle of Love

Stephanie S. Smith

My husband will be coming home soon and I am kneading sweet dough with honey for our dinner. I am still finding my way around the kitchen, a new bride just cracking open white-ribboned boxes of waffle irons and espresso cups fresh from our wedding registry. Cooking is alien territory for me, one that I am eagerly exploring, but a strange landscape nonetheless because it reinforces the foreign fact that I am a wife. A work-from-home, domestic, dinner-making… wife.

They say the bedroom is the theatre of conflict for most couples, but for us, it is the kitchen. I expect Zach to do his share of the dishwashing. It gets under my skin when he sits leisurely at the table talking with me while I am poised at the stove, though I certainly don't want his help either. I turn suddenly sensitive, suspicious when the clean-up falls to me, as if a dangerous cue of domestic deference.

The dough is too wet and my patience is thin. I roll up my sleeves in frustration and slip my wedding band and engagement ring, sixteen diamonds set like a star, into a teacup near the sink. I've learned the hard way to take them off when I work with dough, lest the diamond glow cloud over with milky white. The last time I attempted homemade pizza dough—simple enough I had supposed— turned out to be a disaster. Zach, observing my distress, had gently offered to take me out for dinner instead, but I flatly refused. I had not come this far for flour to confound me.

But it's never about the meal. A woman in the kitchen, I fear that my path has already been cut out for me, without my permission or will, and that I will be cast according to our nation's generationally ingrained pattern of subdued and voiceless women. In the kitchen, I gracelessly project onto my husband the religious and cultural molds I have long resisted. And all of this I do on the offense — without Zach ever giving me a single reason on which to found my fears.

I set our tiny apartment table for two with the silverware we picked out together, recalling how such silverware sparked a memorable argument between my parents approaching their own wedding. My mother thought three-tined forks elegant; my father frowned upon their impracticality. In the end, they tied the knot just the same. My mother kept her maiden name as she had wanted, and they ordered a silver set with four-tined forks. They've been happily married for 33 years.

The women of my family tree have always possessed a certain flair for breaking out of stereotypes. First there's my mother, who answers to no name but her own. My grandmother, who is as blonde and blue-eyed as they come, won the "Best Woman of the Year" award for her work with Meals on Wheels in Baltimore — from an African-American sorority. My lineage is filled with women who were college valedictorians when it was rare for women to get degrees at all, who led troops of war ambulances (and repaired them!) in ankle-length skirts, who founded non-profits, traveled the world to countries I'd never heard of nor could pronounce, and all of whom loved and cared for their husbands and children.

Then I, the middle child of three daughters, enrolled in a Bible college that had rules about when, how, and where a woman could teach God's Word. I surprised myself by switching my major to Women's Ministry, and I began studying gender and faith with fascination while at the same time wrestling to reject the suspicion that I was the daughter of a God who had wished for a son.

Little did I know that just a few months beyond my Women's Ministry college career I would find these concepts of male and female design taking on a whole new face. Because in married life, it eats across from me at the table, kisses me in the morning when I wake up, buys me popcorn at the movies. I was jaded after studying ad nauseam the tangled controversies surrounding men and women, female ordination and obscure Greek words, headship and submission. I craved a reintroduction, and what finally spoke to me was a story.

Just as I was discovering the world of cooking as a newlywed, spooning local honey onto our bread, making my first chicken pot pie, I picked up a copy of *The Secret Life of Bees*. In this imaginative novel, Sue Monk Kidd creates a world in which Black Madonnas are worshipped, male bees have no purpose except to procreate with the queen, and marriage is wrestled over as a potential threat to personhood. At first, Kidd's novel seems to embody the antithesis of Christian gender orthodoxy, but against this golden backdrop of beekeeping sisters I gained a greater sense of the true feminine form.

The story is about a runaway girl searching for answers about her deceased mother, a quest which takes Lily and her nanny away from her abusive father and into the refuge of three African-American sisters. The sisters lead an unconventional life, harvesting honey which they label with the icon of a Black Madonna, the image of which resides in their living room: an old ship's figurehead said to have delivered slaves to their freedom. The sisters revere her as "Our Lady of Chains" not because she wore them, they triumphantly remind each other, but because she *broke* them.

I was tired of the straw woman clichés I encountered as a student of gender roles, the doormat housewife, the power-hungry prima donna, neither of which I hoped to emulate. And as I read *The Secret Life of Bees*, I found myself drawn to the Black Madonna's bold and balanced portrait of femininity displayed in her wooden skin: bearing both a red-painted heart, an emblem of her maternal love, and a dark, raised fist, a mark of her courage.

Despite biblical descriptions and gilded icons, I have never quite known how to picture Mary. I see her as purity personified, the archetype of the Christian feminine ideal. A pastel face under a blue hood. Sue Monk Kidd articulated my very thoughts as she once confessed, "…Mary and sacred feminine images in general had become wounded, diminished, and sacrificed… I was put off by the meek and mild look. I wanted to shake her."[7] Instead, Kidd was moved to create the Black Madonna of her novel by legends

---

7   Sue Monk Kidd, *Traveling with Pomegranates* (New York: Penguin Books, reprint edition 2010), 48.

of the holy mother who favored more subversive graces, such as forgiving heretics destined for burning at the stake and rescuing unbaptized babies from Limbo [194].

I began to see a heroine in the Black Madonna of *The Secret Life of Bees,* and likewise in the young girl who birthed a God herself. For she too had a red-painted heart—the gospels tell us Mary treasured in her heart thoughts about her Child King. And although the virgin mother is more likely to be pictured with hands clasped in prayer than with raised fists, she also possessed courage and strength. Strength enough to bear the sword that would piece her heart, as the prophet Simeon foretold her. Courage enough to bear social ostracism for her unexpected pregnancy, poverty, political exile for the protection of her family, and, most of all, the pain of watching the son of her womb being torn, beaten, and bruised.

"She is a muscle of love, this Mary," say the sisters in *The Secret Life of Bees,*[8] a tender warrior, "a mix of mighty and humble all in one."[9] I am still working out this delicate dance of male and female design, trying to redeem the harmony I truly believe was once beautiful before it was cluttered with the shrapnel of Eden as it fell. But thanks to a story of honeycomb and daughters, I have discovered this much: If we have a heart without a fist, we may become voiceless and vulnerable; if we have a fist without a heart, we may become bitter, belligerent souls.

The dough has finally become soft, a pale cloud in my hands. I shoulder my weight into it, the mound indenting at my touch, inflating at my release, and it lets loose a revelation of honey into the air.

I have wrestled with my new role as a married woman, and I have wrestled with dough. It can be sticky, frustrating, knotting between my fingers in uncooperative clumps. But tonight I sink contentedly into the rhythm of kneading, enjoying this handmade process and anticipating the company of my love over a good meal. I brush the flour from my sleeves, return my rings to the hand where they belong, and slide the dough into the oven—knowing that it will soon nurture us both.

---

8   Sue Monk Kidd, *The Secret Life of Bees* (New York: Penguin Books, 2001), 302.
9   Ibid, 70.

Good Enough

Amy Nabors

I remember sitting in cloth-covered pews feeling out of place—feeling as if I weren't perfect enough to earn salvation. I spent my school days sitting in desks lined up in a row, never feeling as if I quite fit in—never feeling good enough.

I'm not sure when my expectation of perfection began. My home life was good with parents who loved me and a grandfather who adored me. My parents worked hard to provide us with much they never had; we were not well off, but we had all we needed and then some. My adoring grandfather imparted his love of music to me as I sat with him at his old upright piano—and his fiddle. How I loved that fiddle. Life was almost idyllic with plenty of wide open space and country air. The Appalachian foothills surrounded the valley I called home. Cows grazed in pastures across the road and tall trees shaded our days of play.

For most of my childhood years we had an artificial tree for Christmas. It looked as close to real as any artificial tree you could find. But I dreaded the weekend it went up. My sister and I would spend hours with our mother standing around the tree, pulling and fluffing out each branch and twig to make it look just so. Perfection.

Life was almost idyllic—almost. My beloved grandfather passed away a few months before my eleventh birthday, his body finally succumbing to cancer. Two months after his death, my mother was diagnosed with an autoimmune disease and spent the next three years in and out of hospitals.

Even before my mother's illness, I always had a personality that carried the weight of the world. So at eleven I played the role of big sister well—watching out after my sister and making us dinner (as much of a dinner as an eleven-year-old can prepare) when we were allowed to stay home for a few hours under the watchful eyes of our next-door neighbors. I wanted everything to be perfect. Perfect so my mother would not worry. Perfect so she could get better.

Perhaps our small country churches compounded my expectation to be perfect—at least the message my childhood mind perceived did. Sermons spewing the evils of everything from alcohol to sex were the norm, and, with my sensitive nature, I felt guilt even though those aspects of life were distant. I never sensed grace. I grappled with unattainable rules. Rules I was not even old enough to break.

Of course I had always been told God loved me. I knew I was "fearfully and wonderfully made," but knowing in my head was different from knowing in my heart. So I learned to wear the mask of perfection early, and I kept it on. Through my teen years, through college, and into marriage, I strove to do everything perfectly so I wouldn't let anyone down. So no one would worry. So everyone would like me. And I allowed expectations, some real and others perceived, to smother who God created me to be.

Striving for perfection came at a price. If I felt I could not do something perfectly the first time, I would not do it. If I thought I might fail, I refused to try. I thought I would never be good enough, so why bother? When I did try and fail, I allowed it to devastate me. Fear of failure—of rejection—kept me from putting the work into becoming better at many things I loved. Music, singing, writing— all tempered with fear.

For so many years my heart believed perfection equaled worth. And then my son entered my life. Motherhood forced me to peel away the expectations of myself that I carried. Toys lay scattered about and laundry piled up. Our toddler never behaved how I expected. It was all a picture of how I felt: never perfect or good enough. Something had to go. When I gave up on perfection, God began writing on my heart my true worth.

Through my son, through photography, and through art, God brushed away my skewed perceptions. I released expectations I had of myself as well as expectations I perceived others had placed on me.

I watched as my son sat drawing for hours on our driveway, his toddler hands moving chalk around the concrete, forming what he saw in his mind. He sketched cities, characters, and places and then acted out his imaginary scenes, never caring if anyone was watching. Never caring if it was good enough or if his drawings met perfection.

As he grew, so did his artistic abilities. This gift God blessed him with evident, we knew we needed to invest in his talents. And as he began taking art lessons, a quiet voice pushed me to learn alongside him.

In the beginning, my fingers painted pastels onto paper just as he did. Soon I brushed acrylic onto canvas. With photography, I attempted to capture the beauty I saw in front of me. As I painted, as I photographed, I began letting go of the fear that what I created was not good enough. I looked at what I created and it was good because I created it.

And God whispered, "You are good enough because I created you." His truth slowly redefined my worth through it all. His grace covered me so I did not have to be perfect.

Lies try to worm their way back into my mind more often than I would like. When they do, I have learned to push back, drowning them with God's truth: "I am fearfully and wonderfully made." When lies overwhelm my thoughts, comparing me to others who paint better, photograph better, parent better, I remind them He engraved me on the palms of His hands, so why should I compare myself to others? When I make mistakes and feel the weight of imperfection take hold, I push it away knowing "His grace is sufficient for me." There are days when comparison threatens to dictate who I am. Some days the lies win, but I am learning to capture those thoughts and fight back with the truth God gives. His promises, His grace, and His love, my weapons against the lies and fear that I am not good enough.

We should strive to do our best, but when we put such pressure on ourselves for perfection, we lose sight of our true worth. Because perfectionism teaches us to compare ourselves to others, humanity's view of perfection strips us of our worth and suffocates who God created us to be. I've learned that humanity's definition of *perfect* twists how God sees perfection, distorting our understanding of how God values each of us. I've learned to tune out the voices that want me to believe I must perform to earn my worth. Fighting against this skewed perception takes practice, patience, and time.

But now, at least most days, the pressures of perfection no longer define me. God sees me through the perfection of Christ. And that is all I need to define my worth.

The Weight of Shame

Lindsay Holifield

Shame. I first felt shame—the feeling that I was, deep down, not good enough—when I was nine years old, and I have felt it ever since.

The seed of shame and self-hatred took root when I was very young. I grew up in a fundamentalist Christian home where God's judgment and wrath were emphasized. I knew all the things I needed to do to keep God happy and I also knew, too well, all of the ways that I failed to do that. The weight of those rules was unbearable on a young girl, but I tried with everything I had to keep all of them perfectly. With each successive failure, a new layer of guilt and shame formed. I confessed my sins compulsively to my family and to God, but nothing I did was ever enough to rid myself of the feeling that I was a failure to God. Later, though I wouldn't know it for a long time, a counselor gave a name to my experiences: spiritual abuse.

The relationship I had with my sister also sent me messages of shame. My sister is two years older than me, but even though we were not far apart in age, we couldn't have been more distant in our relationship. I remember watching my friends who had siblings and being jealous of how close they seemed. Instead of being affectionate, our relationship was one of anger and hate. I wanted my sister's attention so badly, but she treated me like I was nothing; there are no words to describe how much it hurts to be rejected by your own sister. The shame began whispering to me that if my own sister hated me, I must be terribly broken.

In school settings, my introversion kept me from reaching out to make friends. The lack of close relationships felt like another confirmation that I was broken. Each time I sat by myself at a lunch table or recess, I became more and more convinced that there was something fundamentally wrong with me. I became convinced that the reason no one wanted to be friends with me was that I was not pretty enough, thin enough, or athletic enough. And no one told me I was wrong—no one told me that I was not dirty or ugly or bad. No one told me that I had nothing to be ashamed of. And so I believed in the shame.

Middle school, in all its awkwardness, was especially painful. My body was changing and I grew extremely self-conscious— I was aware that I was not the image on the magazine cover. My best friend moved away in the midst of this transition, and I felt more alone than ever. As my family was extremely involved in church, I was at every event. But I sat by myself and pretended like the group of girls laughing didn't matter to me. Although during the day I kept up that lie, I would cry myself to sleep at night, desperate to stop being invisible.

At the same time, my parents were telling me to be "the salt and the light" to my friends. I was to let them know that their sinful behavior—like watching certain movies, cussing, or wearing immodest clothing—was wrong and that God didn't want them live that way. My parents told me that living for Jesus would mean that people might not like me but that I was called to be righteous and holy. When the loneliness hit, I tried to tell myself that God was proud of me, but it did nothing to erase the pain. I blamed myself for being different and, in my mind, so unlikable.

As I entered high school, my body was stretching out, starting to make sense of itself. I found a group of "friends," people with whom I would laugh at the right moments and go to the right events. The mask I wore to fit in kept the true me well hidden. I didn't think that girl deserved to be seen or heard. She wasn't good enough. I didn't date, probably because I was so quiet that no one knew me well, and it made me hate myself even more.

My sophomore year in high school, after years of feeling powerless about the inadequacies I saw in my body, I made a New Year's resolution to "get healthier." I knew, really, that it was not for the sake of my health, but a drive to be thinner and hopefully get the acceptance I craved from my peers. I started out jogging and choosing foods with fewer calories, but the power I got from seeing the number on the scale go down was intoxicating. Soon, I was barely eating anything. By April, I was hospitalized for six weeks for severe malnutrition and dehydration. It was the first time I was diagnosed with anorexia nervosa.

The hospital got me healthier physically, but it didn't deal with what was underneath. A few months later, I relapsed. My parents forced me into a treatment program and I faked my way through; two months later I returned exactly the same.

The darkness of depression now followed me everywhere, and my junior year, I started cutting myself. For some reason, it felt right—I deserved to be punished.

As I continued to starve myself, the little voice in my head kept whispering that no matter how miserable it made me, I had to keep going. It made me someone special and helped me feel okay about my body for once in my life. At the same time, it was the punishment I believed I deserved for not being good enough for God, my friends, or my family. I would pray each night to not wake up in the morning. Finally, when I was barely able to get out of bed each day because my body was shutting down, I asked to go back to treatment.

During that time I had still been going to church, but the leaders made it clear that I was sinning and needed to repent. I was told that terrible things could happen to people I cared about because of my sin. More guilt. More shame. I stopped going to church for a while because I couldn't pretend to be the girl they wanted me to be. That mask was getting tiring. The very place that should have offered me grace was condemning me.

My church failed me, but when I went to treatment in the summer after my junior year, God met me through one of my counselors. This woman spoke to me of things I had never heard before. Instead of telling me that I was a worthless sinner, she spoke about grace and love from a God who didn't see me as dirty. She was the first person who showed me what unconditional love looked like. Her words started to break the walls around my heart. But each time she said those words, I would shake my head and tell her, "No, it's not possible." I pushed away this love, but it wouldn't leave me alone. When I expected shame, she showed me grace. She showed me Jesus.

I came home not fully believing her words but with the tiniest spark of hope beginning to burn in my heart. But the next few months were some of the darkest in my life. My family relationships were dysfunctional, and I began to cut daily. Depression was suffocating. I was barely surviving.

Just as I was beginning to feel more and more desperate, I visited a church nearby with a friend. I didn't expect much — after all, I had grown up in church. My mom taught Bible studies and I had studied the Bible myself since I was young. This was nothing new. But there was something different about this church. The staff noticed me, they welcomed me, and they were loving toward me. I started to attend regularly.

I connected with one of the leaders in the youth ministry, and she walked alongside me through some of the days I wasn't sure I would make it. She told me about my worth and value and how God saw me, over and over again. She never let up, and more than just speaking words, she showed me through her actions that she believed I mattered.

I wish I could say I suddenly believed her and took care of myself, but that wouldn't be true. I continued to struggle with the eating disorder, and in the spring of my senior year, I attempted suicide. While my parents drove me to the hospital, I held my phone to my ear and called the youth leader. I stayed on the line with her the whole time, and she assured me she was there for me. Her words of comfort got me through the next few rough days.

In the fall, I left for college, and over the next couple of years not much changed. Some days I would eat, others I wouldn't, and most of the time I lived in a haze. Life was a miserable grey. Somewhere amid this haze, I began purging. It felt like taking every dirty part of me and forcing it out, cleansing myself. I longed to feel clean, to feel accepted and loved. When I ate well, I felt like I had done what God wanted; when I messed up, He was disappointed. I lived in a constant cycle of self-condemnation for not measuring up.

Before my junior year of college, I was lying to everyone I knew to hide the eating disorder. I had become skilled at keeping secrets, but it was exhausting. So I decided to do a brave, scary thing: I decided that I would go to treatment again. I felt like a failure not to be able to conquer this myself, but I was growing weary of the torture I was putting myself through.

Change doesn't happen until we are ready. That summer, I was ready for something new. I remember my counselor telling me to pretend my nine-year-old self was sitting across from me, the shame-filled, quiet girl who was never enough. She asked me to tell her what I would have wanted to hear. The moment I opened my mouth, I broke down. When the sobs subsided, I was able to get out the words, little by little.

"You were okay just the way you were."

"You didn't have to be 'good enough.'"

"You weren't dirty."

"You were so, so loved."

Each time, it was as if something were breaking inside of me. I don't know if I've ever cried quite so hard. That night, I lay in bed, my heart lighter than it had been in a long, long time. I was beginning to see that although I couldn't change the pain and hurt I had experienced growing up, I could take care of that little girl now. I could love her, and cherish her, and tell her she was beautiful. Little by little, I began to believe the truth.

It didn't all happen in that one night. It is a process, and it is still a challenge every day to wake up and believe that I am worth loving as I am. But I believe it a tiny bit more each time I choose the truth that I am unconditionally loved over the lie of shame. And every day, I am discovering God; not the angry God I grew up with who was fickle with His affection, but my good Father. He was the voice that whispered through the people in my life who showed me love. He was the glimpse of hope when I wanted to die. He was the one who held me when the pain was too much.

He is the one who delights in me today and every day, just as I am.

Private Lessons

Kara Gause

You're only, what, 18 or 19, right? You don't know anything yet. You don't know how the world really works. You missed a once-in-a-lifetime opportunity here. What happened — if it happened at all — is nothing in the grand scheme of things. You'll come to regret this.

So said the dean to the 19-year-old student.

I was used to people putting their hands on me. As a child actor, logging serious hours in dance studios, private voice lessons, and countless stages meant hands were always on me. Someone was always adjusting and tweaking, putting my body into place.

Head up! Shoulders back. Derrière tucked. Hips under. Feet rotated out — from the hips! Breathe from the diaphragm. Project! Emote! Reach! Stretch!

I could belt out a standard from a Broadway show in nothing flat, recite a monologue to order, complete with Cockney accent— or Southern, if you preferred— and of course, I could offer up a little soft shoe or a grand jeté. *Just let me entertain you! Give me your approval. Tell me I'm good enough.*

The shy girl— whose parents had tentatively placed her in ballet class to gain some self-confidence— had learned to engage an audience. Back then, I was most eager to please those who taught and directed me. Their expert opinion meant the world to me. To this day, I sometimes catch myself morphing into what I think people want me to be, reciting the lines I know they want to hear. It's a habit I still struggle to break.

So I sang and danced my way through childhood and all the way to college. All my hard work was rewarded with a full scholarship into a large university theatre program, something too unbelievably wonderful to me. I'd been so focused on pleasing whomever the nameless judge or director or teacher happened to be, I honestly never considered there might be any real talent in me. All that work and no joy! But now I had a scholarship, a trophy of sorts, which meant maybe I did have promise. Maybe I could even make good on it.

Just two weeks into my college experience I was buoyant. I was hopeful. I was happy. *They like me! They really like me!* On a whim, I auditioned for a voice minor scholarship in the music department and was thrilled when a doctoral candidate handpicked me as his student.

I remember what I wore that day to what would be my first and only private lesson with the teacher. I would question those shorts over and over again. Were they too short? Was my striped t-shirt too tight? Was the shade of red on my toenails too provocative? Was I asking for it?

The room was small to begin with, but shoving two pianos and two desks into it made for especially close quarters between student and teacher. He led me through my vocal-eases, his hands just inches from my legs.

Do you have a boyfriend? The teacher brushed my thigh with his fingertips, feeling me out. What kind of student was I? Would I play along?

A pretty girl like you, I'll bet you have a boyfriend. Oh, you do, huh?

My Do-Re-Mis were unacceptable. Twelve years of training and yet, somehow, my breath control was insufficient for this teacher. He got up from the piano.

He had me against the wall now, his hand against my rib cage, slipping one, two fingers under the stripes. Why was this uncomfortable for me now? There had been other teachers before him. Other hands had touched my rib cage, adjusted my positioning.

Push your diaphragm out against my hand. Harder. His breath was hot against my ear but his touch absolutely frigid as he cupped my breast.

Wait—*had* he touched my breast?

Obedient: That's the kind of student I was. I was naïve and trusting, and I was still more girl than woman as he slid his hand from my waist down between my legs.

My mind raced to make sense of what was happening to me. A voice croaked answers to his prompts of breath control as his hands took their control over me. I was frozen while his hands took and grabbed and stole things. I'm still looking for some of those things today.

I barely noticed when the door opened abruptly. Though my ears were ringing, I heard a male student apologize— he had the wrong room. He stumbled over his words. I often wonder at the scene he walked in on. What it must have looked like to him!

But it was enough. That brief interruption broke my obedience, and it broke his hold over me. I don't know what I said to get out of that damn room, but I said it and literally ran.

I ran all the way across campus, not stopping. I didn't notice my tears until I opened the door to my dorm room where my new roommate was on the phone with my mother; she'd called worried about my lesson. Mother's intuition had her worried something had gone wrong.

Something *was* gone. *So* much was wrong.

Private voice lessons are overrated. That's what I'd said when I dropped my voice scholarship. But I still saw the teacher everywhere. With our departments in the same building, he'd show up after one of my classes to chat up another professor. He'd smile to leave, then turn and force my eyes to meet his.

There were rumors of more female students. Fingers pointed and tongues wagged, though I had yet to tell anyone my own story. Still, you don't just give up a scholarship after one lesson.

Slowly, I became a student again, though now instead of seeking the spotlight on stage, I found solace behind the scenes, constructing costumes. I threw auditions, no longer wanting an audience. My circle of friends became smaller. Gone was the boyfriend.

I avoided all men at all costs. Male checkout clerks— forget it. I bit my lip and cried while riding an elevator alone with a male student. Tears came constantly, nonsensically. I was fading away and not soon enough for my own liking. What was left for me to do but barter with a God I'd only heard rumor of?

If you get me through the rest of the year without shedding another tear, I'm yours. Do this for me, and I'll do whatever you want.

And the tears stopped. I was numb and tense and scared to death of men, but the tears did stop. I could manage the rest of the school year. After my last spring semester exam, I promptly walked to my little Ford station wagon, manually locked all the doors from inside, and heaved sobs.

This God person continued to show up and hold me together until one day I felt life moving forward again. Moving on for me meant transferring to another university. All that remained was an exit interview to relinquish my theatre scholarship. Thankfully, the Dean of Theatre was kind and gentle and gay. Otherwise, I would have been an absolute wreck.

I had nothing to left to lose, so I told him exactly why I was leaving. With every word, I felt lighter letting go of my secret. The burden of it had weighed me down and isolated me to the point where I hardly knew myself anymore. Speaking was an unexpected release.

Naturally, my sweet Dean of Theatre was appalled and insisted I meet with his colleague, the Dean of Music, immediately — let him know what was going on under his own roof. But his colleague was not kind, nor was he gentle.

Your teacher is a fine musician, known the world over. He's brought us a great deal of prestige and clout. Are you absolutely sure this is what really happened?

I told him I was sure. *I was sure, wasn't I?* That's when the Dean of Music decided to school me.

You're only, what, 18 or 19, right? You don't know anything yet. You don't know how the world really works. You missed a once-in-a-lifetime opportunity here. What happened — if it happened at all — is nothing in the grand scheme of things. You'll come to regret this.

I haven't regretted it, but I have continued to doubt myself. Encouraged by the Dean of Theatre to testify against the teacher along with another five female students, I second-guessed my own actions — not the teacher's. I certainly questioned my own value. Was it talent or weakness that had appealed to him in that audition? I don't think I'll ever know.

To this day I'll wait an extra 10 minutes for the female checkout clerk, thanks very much. I just chuckle to myself, perhaps a little bitterly, and wait my turn. There's no mistaking it: My "education" all those years ago has changed me. It beat me up with its rough edges and made me feel filthy, less-than. It left its deep, wide, indelible mark. It shook my world to its core in such a way that I was forced to look up and outside of it.

But isn't that the point? Our experiences aren't frivolous. Whether we choose them or strangers in a small, suffocating room force them upon us, they leave a patina. They tell a story about a God who waits to meet us in the middle of searing pain and great shame. Hope is born in these moments.

It was in my despair that I met Jesus. One thing I've come to know about my Savior is that he uses everything— all circumstances, each sorrow— for his purposes. Nothing is wasted, not one tear.

My circumstances were not a surprise for Jesus, and he used them for my good. Still on scholarship with the theater department, I was appointed an upperclassman mentor with the same scholarship. She was a Christ-follower, and it was mandatory that I spend time with her. Because of that friendship, the God who had been an acquaintance to me as a child became a friend and comforter. For the first time, I heard and began to understand God's promises of a heavenly home, of rescue from this world where we hurt each other.

While my world spun and flailed and whipped uncontrollably around me, God became my axis— my True North. He made my life and this experience mean something. They weren't a waste. I wasn't a waste. When one man tried to make me out as nothing more than a plaything, God stepped in to show me otherwise: I am priceless, someone worth singing about.

"The LORD your God is with you, the Mighty Warrior who saves. He will take great delight in you; in his love he will no longer rebuke you, but will rejoice over you with singing." -Zephaniah 3:17

A Letter to my Daughters

Sarah Bessey

My girls,

Here are the lies:

> *You are only as good as you look.*
>
> *You can conquer your feelings of inadequacy by being skinny.*
>
> *Nothing tastes as good as skinny feels.*
>
> *Everyone judges you by how you look.*
>
> *You are not beautiful.*
>
> *You are only valuable if you are beautiful or productive.*
>
> *You are not worthy of love.*

I'm raising you in a world that thinks women are only as good as they look. And you're being raised by a woman who is still overcoming these lies herself.

One day, I did an exercise video at home. You were with me, Anne, while the two littlest ones slept and we leaped and kicked our way through jumping-jacks together. "Oh, Mum!" you glowed, "Even your tummy is having fun! Look at it jumping around!" and for a moment, oh, it stung. I had given birth to Evelynn two months before and so yes, my tummy was "jumping around," and part of me wanted to sit down and cry for the sudden cacophony of worthlessness and shame that rose up but then *you were there*. You were there, looking up at me (you always are) and I thought, *No.*

No, I will not cry about how I look in front of you. I will not give you that memory. Instead I told you that yes, my tummy was having a marvellous time. When you asked me why we were exercising, I had to lock my lips tight against the "to lose weight because I'm fat" that threatened to spill out and instead spoke of having fun exercising for energy and playing together to be healthy and strong and hey, later, did you want to go bike riding?

I promised when you were a toddler to look out for the small ways to spare you just a few battles of body-image that seem to strangle and entangle so many of us, to guard against the grief of chaining your worth to your appearance. On that day, a few years ago, I went to my closet to dig out my work clothes. It had been two years since I had to wear a pair of dress pants and you know what?

They didn't fit.

I tried on another pair of pants. Then a blouse. Then another pair of pants. Then another bra. Nothing fit quite right. Buttons were straining, zippers weren't closing. And it was an awful feeling.

Then I tried on my shoes. And I'll be damned if even my *shoes* didn't fit. Evidently, thanks to the latest pregnancy, I'd gone from a 7 1/2 to an 8. Not a pair of shoes in my closet other than my beat-up Converse runners fit.

I cried.

You see, it's always been a sore spot for me (isn't it for all of us?). I was a skinny, leggy kid that turned into a curvy girl overnight. A curvy girl with a strikingly thin and beautiful mother and sister. I was galumphing along, volunteering for the back row. Even at my thinnest, I felt like A Big Girl, unbeautiful, unworthy.

I battled for years with those very culture lie-songs, set on repeat, that sang into my ears, a mix tape of You're fat and ugly...if only you were skinnier....if only you were prettier....if only you weren't so heavy...you're disgusting....everyone is judging you.

The playlist was on full repeat and at a frighteningly loud level of volume. I was probably just as angry over the fact that I was hating it. After all, wasn't I past this? Am I not a child of the King? Am I not enough of a feminist to not care that my thighs touch at the top? At the end of my life, will I really care that I was 20 pounds overweight? Am I not happily married to a man that finds me beautiful? Is my appearance the measure of a life?

Of course not. I knew better.

But I didn't.

But I do.

But I don't.

You all came in and sat on the bed. So I pulled it together, wiped my tears and, with the air of one on a supremely distasteful task, finished dressing. I settled for a pair of jeans that gave me the smallest muffin-top, then stood there, loathing myself.

I had never felt more matronly, more frustrated, more old and fat and ugly than at that moment.

"You look so beautiful, Mummy."

There was your voice from the bed. Your eyes were on me. You'd spoken up with your pudgy, then-three-year-old hands clasped in front of you, adoring.

"You are so beautiful."

Now? Right now? At this moment?

"We are *pretty ladies*," you said proudly. "We are lovely."

Your dad's eyes were fastened on me as well — he knew. He looked at me with one bushy eyebrow raised.

"That's what I keep telling you both," he said.

He reached out and touched my waist, hand resting on my silvery stretch marks.

"Beautiful, Sarah. *Beautiful.*"

Your dad kindly asked me to never say those things in front of you again. He didn't want you to grow up hearing your mother say those things, teaching you by example. So I promised him. You will have your own battles to wage, your own song to write, my dears. I do not wish to send you into the world already distracted by your mother's broken tunes.

So sure, I will talk and teach and train but I am learning this: You will sing my songs.

And so I will sing a song of wonder and beauty about womanhood for you to learn from my lips. And I will believe it myself to my bones. I will lead the resistance of these lies in our home by living out a better truth.

I will not criticise my sisters for how they look or live, casting uncharitable words like stones, because my words of criticism or judgement have a strange way of being more boomerang than idle gossip, swinging around to lodge in your own hearts.

I'll wear a bathing suit and I won't tug on it self-consciously. I will get my hair wet.

I will easily change my clothes in front of your dad, proud of my stretch marks that gave us a family, of breasts that nourished his babies. I won't apologise for aging.

I will prove to you that you can be a size 14 and still be sexier than hell. I will prove to you that you don't have to be all angles and corners, that there is room for some softness. I will not let the words "I'm fat" cross my lips.

I will eat dessert and raise my wine glass and laugh my way to deeper smile lines.

I will celebrate your own beauty, my girls, yes, but I will do my best to praise your mind, your heart, your motives as much as I praise your beauty.

I will celebrate beauty where I find it, in a million faces uniquely handcrafted by a generous God with a big tent of glorious womanhood. I will tell stories and surround you with a community of good women, and you will see that this is what is beautiful, that a generous love is the most gorgeous thing you could ever put on.

I'll trace the line of time backwards for you until you see the women that came before you in a great cloud of witnesses for your life. Not to burden you, small pixies, but to empower you. After all, there are hard-working, brave, crazy, passionate blood-women pulsing in that heart of yours and you took in their guts and soul with your mother's milk.

We are thumping along with you, out here in the world now, reminding you that you are fearfully and wonderfully made. And you have a voice and a reason for being. You have a future and a hope. Know who you are, small girls, and when you forget, we'll remind you. You are already girls after God's own heart.

Above all, be a woman who loves.

How am I so blessed as to raise you all up into womanhood? Your own stories will be a beautiful thing to see unfold and I'm privileged for my front-row seat. You have helped me to see every other mother in the world with walls-crumbling-down eyes; every little girl has your face and now it's not enough to raise you well to a suburb with a mini-van to go to church on Sunday and pay your taxes. I am learning the counter-cultural in my own life and sowing it with prayer into yours. A life that tells a story of love because every girl could be you, every mama could be me, and every woman could be us, so we speak up, we pray, we sow our seed in hope and faith, we sing our worth out loud for our own ears to hear.

One day, Anne, we sat together and you asked me if I remembered when you were a baby and how we used to make each other laugh. I think you must have been looking at old pictures of that happening, but who knows? Maybe you do remember. And I said, "Yes, yes, I do remember that."

And you said, "We loved each other right from the start, didn't we?"

Yes, yes we did. We were all loved, right from the start.

Love, Mum

Part 5: Am I Whole?

Stories of Faith

Introduction

Tamára Lunardo

Broken to Fix You

I trace your story
across your face,
and I want to rewrite,
but I read.

I am too broken
to fix you.

I feel your wounds
with heart and hands,
but mine can't heal,
just hold.

I am too broken
too.

So I lift stories
and hearts and wounds
as whispers and cries
in God's ear.

I am too broken
to fix you.

I beg it's enough
to make you whole,
that He was broken
to fix you.

I am too broken
too.

***

I was a theoretical Christian. I could believe against all logic that a perfect God-man died and went to Hell, returned to Earth, and then went to Heaven. I just couldn't believe he did it for me.

I knew God was a Father, and I knew that for some people, he was loving and tender and close. But my first father had left me and my second had hated me. So for me, he was disapproving and harsh and distant. There was a lifetime of shame separating me from a perfect, holy God.

I lived — but then, not really — in the oppressive thick of depression. I was a ghost of a woman, empty, longing for substance, listless for a life that I no longer believed I had any hope of having. I knew my story — I was a wasted creative, an insubordinate, a thing to fuck, an unfavored child.

My husband was kind and supportive, but his care was not enough to pull me from the mire. My children were lights, but I could not enter into their brilliance with joy. I could laugh with friends, but on my own, the only way to stop the tears was to sleep. So I slept, but I found no rest, and I could scarcely wake.

Writing was how I lived — not how I made a living, but how I was made alive — but I no longer had energy to open my heart on the page. My heart was too heavy, so I just shut it down, away from the people I loved and the work I loved and the God I wanted to love. And in that closed-up darkness, I found I was profoundly alone.

And when I was alone, really alone, there was nothing but me and my thick cloud of shame, and all I could do was sit with myself in it. And the thing about shame is you really can't get out of it from the inside; you have to be rescued by something stronger outside it.

And love is the only thing I know that's stronger than shame.

I had gotten to know about God without knowing God. And I knew I needed to know him, even if a father was a forbidding thing to know. So I read the stories of Jesus. And I began not to just know about him, but to know him. He was funny and tender, piercing and radically good. He loved people who didn't belong, women who had been used til they believed they had no use, and he got close, uncomfortably close, so people had no choice but to run away or to melt right into him. And I melted. I began to love Jesus in a way I'd never loved another man because he loved me in a way no other man had ever loved me.

But still, God was a father, and I feared what he thought of me. I feared we could never be close because I could never be worth getting close to. And one night, I was wracked with tears and terror, with longing and shame, and I needed my mother. I needed her comforting hair strokes and her gentle voice and her strong arms. But it was the middle of the night and I was a grown woman. So I thought of Jesus and the way he said he wanted to gather his people together like a mother hen, and I asked God through exhausted tears if please, even just for the night, he would be a mother to me.

And I did not get a loud miraculous answer, but I got rest, and that was miracle enough.

Soon it was Lent, a season of relinquishment, and I decided that what I needed to give up was "God." I needed to let go of everything I thought I knew about God so that there would be room in my heart to know God. And in that space, an intimately personal God, one who did not need a gender or even my own goodness in order to be close to me, drew near. And in that tender closeness of a Mother God, I finally understood the story of who I really am: I am God's child.

I no longer feared I was the wrong child, the bad child, the terribly disappointing child, because, for the first time, my ideas were out of the way and my heart could feel the truth. I was the precious child, the beloved child, the worthwhile child.

So in that security, I knew I needed to talk to my dad. He had been demonstrably changing in the many years since I'd left for college, lighter in his heart and gentler in his spirit. We had been doing well, but I had never spoken my deepest heart to him. Now I knew I needed to, and I could. Whatever his reaction, whatever his ability or inability, I would, at the least, have spoken, and he would have heard me.

We sat in my parents' kitchen, my mom at the table with me, and my dad, on a stool at the counter. I said I needed to talk but I faltered, said I couldn't do it.

"Yes you can," he said with full kindness.

So I spoke—I spoke the truth of 33 years and of deepest heart and heartache.

"Dad, I need your attention and acceptance and affection."

He left his stool without hesitation—the father running to greet the prodigal—held me long, and said, "Whatever you need, you just tell me. I want all good things for you. I love you. *You are my daughter*."

And I believed it.

In that moment, I believed I had a dad who saw and loved the real me. Finally, I believed I had his caring attention, his full acceptance, his true affection, not because I had done well or become a perfect version of myself or adhered to certain rules, but because of who I was—his daughter.

And it's funny how things come and move and circle back. Because in that moment of healing with my dad, I could finally allow a tender, safe, secure God to be a Father to me as well. And I could be who I was—and I was whole.

The human heart is always seeking something bigger and better than itself, something to worship, something to make it whole. For many people, this search leads us to religion. But when we seek the answer to the question of our worth in a church, temple, synagogue, or mosque, we find that we are surrounded by people and theology and practices—and these can either lead us to the one true answer to our hearts' desire or distract us thoroughly from it. And so, as the women in this section show through their faith journeys, the key in discovering and believing our true worth is in cutting through all the clutter and simply meeting with the one who established our worth from the very start, the one who makes our hearts whole.

(Not) One of the Boys

Anne Bogel

It's an odd feeling to walk into church on a Sunday morning and be greeted with a warning.

"Watch out, Anne. He's really angry."

I knew he was mad, but I didn't think it would be like this.

After all, it wasn't that big a deal.

***

I grew up in a mainline church with an odd demographical quirk: I was the only girl my age. My little friends Christina and Tomeka moved away in second and third grades, and that left just me—and the boys.

As I moved through the ranks from elementary to middle school, I begged to move up to be with other girls and not stuck with the boys in my own grade. I was repeatedly told, "No." It wouldn't be fair, and it wasn't convenient; it just wasn't possible. I was told I would just have to suck it up and be strong. As a pre-teen girl, I didn't know what it meant to be strong, not like that. So I learned how to survive instead.

It was a male-heavy culture: rowdy boy games, led by a male youth minister whom the teenage boys idolized and imitated. So I made friends with the older girls and hung with them as much as I could, spending many a happy weekend watching *Anne of Green Gables* and drinking tea with these girlfriends. But at church, when we were segregated by grade, I'd do my best to blend in with the boys, to not rock the boat.

It was painful at times. I was trusting and gullible—an irresistible target for pranks. Once, the boys yanked my chair right out from under me at a big church dinner and I landed on the hard gym floor—fork still in hand. I could barely walk for three days. I was complimented for being a "good sport."

I wasn't always a good sport: I objected to a blond joke once and was ridiculed for being "too touchy." So the next time one of the boys outed with, "What do you do when your dishwasher breaks? Hit her!" I cringed inwardly but managed to laugh anyway. So did the youth minister. I even got complimented: "Anne, we love that you laugh at our jokes without getting all mad."

So I kept laughing, playing my part and keeping my mouth shut. I was learning that things went more smoothly when I did.

As we moved into high school, the dynamics started to shift, and it became harder to act like I was just one of the boys. When we returned home from a youth conference on the beach, I started hearing stories about those boys "discovering Anne in her yellow bikini." I missed the older girls who'd gone off to college, leaving me with the boys. I didn't want to deal with boy-girl weirdness at church, especially not without them by my side.

After that summer, I was vaguely aware of talk in the church. I overheard moms muttering to the youth minister in the church hallways things like, "Looks like trouble" and, "Ah, hormones." But I didn't understand what they meant, not yet.

As the school year progressed, occasional comments from my male peers made me think those church moms were on to something, especially where one particular boy was concerned.

"Don't tell him I called you, okay? You know how angry he can get."

"I wish I could date you, but I'm afraid of what he would do."

"He claimed you first."

I had no idea what to say to any of that, so I ignored it or laughed it off so life could continue as normal. It was easy to do—we were 15, 16—nobody was dating much, anyway. And I couldn't imagine they were serious; after all, we were all just buddies. It worked, for a while.

It worked, until *that* boy asked me to a junior class dance. I had known my part; I'd played it well. But I cringed at the thought of going on an actual date with this boy who had "claimed" me, and I wasn't going to play along. We were friends, and that was fine, but the thought of dressing up and putting my arms around his neck and slow dancing was too much to bear—and so I went off script.

I said no.

First he was angry. Then he was mean. And then the rumors started.

I'd been raised to think that if you handled yourself with grace and class, things would take care of themselves. I thought I should hold my head high and be brave because I hadn't done anything wrong. I had wounded his pride, but I thought he'd get over it soon enough.

I was wrong.

The bullying started immediately. I walked through the church doors the next Sunday and was greeted with a warning: "Watch out, Anne. He's really angry." And so he was. There was never any real physical harm, just enough menacing to make me squirm: a heavy backpack dropped on my foot, a body check against the school locker, and always the death stares at church.

The rumors followed close behind. I had always been a good girl, a nice girl, a smart girl. Suddenly, in whispers, I was a drunken slut. I'd walk into church and feel the eyes fixed on me and I'd wonder what everyone had heard and what they believed.

I was comforted by the thought that bullying and false gossip couldn't last long in church, of all places. But the youth minister did nothing, or at least nothing that I knew about. So I sought guidance from his wife, who sighed and said, "Boys will be boys." And those parents who had joked about the trouble brewing in the church hallways—they stood by while I struggled. They didn't know what to do, so they didn't do anything.

And by their inaction, they let the angry boy win.

The school year mercifully ended, but my parents insisted I still go to youth group. Church wasn't a safe place for me anymore—just being there made me nauseated and panicky. I screamed and cried and begged and finally freaked my poor parents out enough that they let me stay home. Shortly after that, they decided it was time to just find a new church.

I was relieved to leave, to start over at a different church where I wasn't always wondering what people thought of me. But I was also ashamed: Why did my male friends support him when they knew he was in the wrong? Why was I the one leaving and not the angry boy? Why was the church supporting him and not me?

When I'd pass an old church friend in the school hallway — one of the younger girls who'd so recently looked up to me — and she'd avert her eyes and walk on by, I'd wonder, *What kind of girl does she think I am?* I wondered if I'd handled it better, whether things would have ended differently. Sometimes I wished I had just said yes and gone to the stupid dance.

After graduation, I took off for a brainy East Coast college. I felt at home in the school, but not in the co-ed dorm. The boys — many of whom were my friends, but *still* — strutted to the shower naked, piled putrid hockey jerseys outside their doors, and hollered porn site recommendations down the halls. It was the last one that killed me. I wanted out of that environment, and fast.

Suddenly, the Christian colleges I had spurned as a high school senior sounded pretty good. When a high school friend convinced me to consider her evangelical school, I flew out for a visit and was accepted as a transfer student.

But that Christian school carried its own form of oppression. I quickly became obsessed with becoming the "right" kind of girl. I read everything I could get my hands on — headship, courtship, women in leadership, women in marriage. What was a Christian woman supposed to be like? I was determined to learn the rules. I didn't see the connection; I didn't realize that brokenness was driving my search.

But I was broken, and I kept circling the pain, blind to its source. "Good-natured" teasing from the pulpit — no matter the target — set my teeth on edge. Discussions of misogyny in the church left me weeping. I had no idea why the topic affected me so profoundly.

That year I started having dreams, and they were always the same: They began with me picking up the phone and calling the boy, and then we'd be at a coffee shop laughing and talking, smoothing away past misunderstanding. I'd apologize for the mess I'd made of things, and we'd hug while my old youth group flooded into the scene.

I'd wake feeling relieved that everyone was on good terms again, but the feeling never lasted. I'd quickly remember that I'd left that group a long time ago, and that those relationships had never been restored. I still felt like damaged goods with that crowd, and I had a nagging sense of guilt that I was responsible. *Why else would I have been the one who had to leave?*

After college, I moved back to my hometown, married a great guy, had a few beautiful kids. But I kept uncovering that old wound. Once or twice a year I'd run into familiar faces from my childhood church and be stricken anew with shame. With each encounter, the memories would come flooding back and my cheeks would burn hot and I'd wonder, *What kind of girl do they think I am? Are they surprised to see me turn out so well? Did they believe those stories back then?*

Every time I'd bump into an old acquaintance, I'd start having those dreams again. But I kept circling the hurt, getting closer to the root, until one day—12 years after telling him no—I woke from a dream with a burst of clarity: That mess wasn't my fault. I had every right to say no, and I couldn't control what happened afterwards. With this new insight, I thought I could finally put it all behind me for good.

My obsession with being a "good" Christian woman continued, but I thought that was normal. I didn't know it was a sign all was not well within.

Five years later on a summer morning, I visited a new church. I was 32. I walked through the door and saw the boy's father and the old shame flared. *Is he surprised I'm in church? What does he think about me? What did he believe about those rumors from back then?*

I came undone. I stumbled into the sanctuary, fighting for composure. The service had already begun, and the preacher was saying something about the Holy Spirit—our counselor. And I thought, *Of course. I needed to see a counselor.* I felt relieved, hopeful. I couldn't believe I'd never thought of that before.

Several weeks later, I went to my first appointment. The counselor asked why I'd come, and I said it was silly, really. The thing I wanted to talk about was so petty and so long ago. It wasn't a big deal.

She said, "Of course it's a big deal — or you wouldn't be here."

She told me I was brave; I didn't quite believe her. But I told her the story of my childhood church and the dance I didn't go to, about what I did (and didn't do) afterwards, and what I wished I'd done differently all those years ago.

My counselor helped me articulate, for the first time, that my pain wasn't just about a dance or a boy — it was about the Church making me feel worthless.

As a teen, I was warned to be on my guard against the media's false messages, which told me my worth came from my sexuality. But no one warned me to guard against false messages I would receive from the Church. I trusted the Church — I naively counted on the Body of Christ to get it right. And when the Church showed me my worth was equal to my compliance, I believed the lie. That lie did more damage than any false message I received from those outside the Church who didn't have my trust.

***

Months after my last counseling session, I dreamt I went to dinner at the boy's house. We were all chatting in the kitchen when he suddenly pointed at me, rolled his eyes, and muttered something to his buddy.

I flared, but not with shame. This time, I strode across the room, hand on hip, and fumed, "You can shut your mouth up right now. You don't know me at all. I am worth more than that." I was done believing the lie of worth-by-compliance.

I said no.

The Sustenance of Words

Cara Sexton

As soon as I was old enough to talk, and though he was never a believer, Dad read me Bible stories as literature. Not the kid-ified ones about Noah's ark and Jonah and the whale but ones out of Revelation, ones about locusts that looked like horses and fiery dragons, about a scarlet beast with seven heads and ten horns.

I thought Christians must be crazy, a sentiment confirmed by my hippie-turned-engineer dad, whose father was a Baptist preacher and mother, a Roman Catholic. Dad was ever disgusted yet fascinated by religion and all the things people told themselves to make this world okay. He had a wall of crosses in his house and took me to Jewish seders and showed me pictures of Islamic mosques. To him, religion was mostly a fanatical reality of this world with a train-wreck sort of appeal, but he reserved a particular and intense disdain for American evangelical Christianity and its brand of blue-eyed Jesus merchandise.

Dad allowed a wide berth for making my own way through life. He believed in exposure and, though I only saw him every-other weekend, he expanded my childhood with travel and philosophy and took me to drag shows and ethnic street fairs and New York City. He bought me a silver lock box when I turned eight, a place to keep my secrets hidden, and promised to never look inside. He told me I could be anything I wanted to be, and when I argued that a woman couldn't be a construction worker or a man, he introduced me to female cement laborers and transvestites, and embroidered my upbringing with feminism before I even knew the word.

When I was too young to read them for myself, Dad read out loud to me late into the night from *Lord of the Rings* and *Lord of the Flies* and *The Iliad* and *The Chronicles of Narnia*, and he opened up my world to the wonder and power of words.

Like most children of divorced parents, I lived a different life during the rest of the calendar days, and the ones I spent at Mom's were far less magical. She worked two jobs and didn't know where her husband hid the vodka, but I did. I tried to be so quiet my stepdad would forget I was home, so I read books in my closet and pretended I was Anne Frank, and I didn't drink all day so I wouldn't have to go to the bathroom, since that's where the vodka was — below the sink, behind the drain cleaner.

The school library became my wonderland and my backpack full of books was my portal to safer places. I'd lug home safe-houses in paperback and huddle under covers and inside pages while outside the bedroom door my stepdad was drunk and stumbling, breaking Mom's ribs and watching John Wayne movies. I learned to hate westerns but love books and the characters within them. And the horrors of this world in print comforted me in my own rocky upbringing. They proved I wasn't alone, just a girl running scared like my friends in *Number the Stars* and *The Diary of Anne Frank* and later in *Go Ask Alice* and *Flowers in the Attic*.

My worth became tangled up in the messages of all the worlds I lived in, skewed by the whispers of here and there like a cosmic game of telephone, ear to ear through all the roles I played: Despised stepdaughter/empowered young female/bookish student/outgoing friend/strong big sister/doormat/confident Girl Scout/punching bag/heartsick admirer/worldly daughter who can be anything she wants to be. The worth-whisper mumbled through my personas, changing shape until nothing remained but nonsense and nothingness.

In books, the story was always linear. Good was good and evil was evil. In life, I learned that people were merely dust and bone, that worth was elusive and assigned by mixed-up adults, all of whom seemed to me a snarled combination of good and bad and everything in between. I figured if Dad was wrong and God was real and especially if God was good, He must be all the while checking marks off a tally sheet to calculate the worth of this girl in the mirror who had no other gauge for calculating value. The God

I'd heard about seemed bent on virtue, and as far as I could tell, I was just too little in all the ways that mattered.

When I was sixteen, I plucked a copy of *All I Need to Know I Learned in Kindergarten* by Robert Fulghum off the shelf in Dad's living room. It might not be the kind of great classic literature that spans generations, but it awakened me to the power of the personal essay, the connection we can make, even across book pages, with other people about the inexcusable, inexplicable, and hysterical nuances of the messy human condition. Reading anecdotes and true stories, I found humor and hope in all the muddy places, laughter and life lessons in paragraph form, poking out between vodka bottles and broken ribs. A great, big revealing light shone in through the cracks of my off-kilter world and I saw for the first time that there was something to be gleaned from all this madness, that if I looked and listened, I could extract jewels from these caverns, jewels that looked like words but shone and sparkled with inspiration and poignancy.

So I fell in love. With Fulghum, with words, with essays, and with writers like Maya Angelou and Anne Lamott, and, right about the same time, with Jesus.

The God my friends knew didn't seem like the one Dad talked about, and when I met Him in person, He turned out not to be a crazy, blue-eyed American deity with a clipboard, but instead, a peaceful presence, a soul-washing Spirit. He was a Whisper louder than all the other whispers in the telephone game, and He told the truth about me, about everybody, about all the tangled up good and evil in the hearts of everyone I'd ever known. And all those roles I'd played relaxed into the only one I needed, even if I was still all those other people. Mostly, I was His.

My weekends with Dad were still full of rich and exciting experiences, and his voice was often the only empowering one I heard. But the way he said *Christian* like his mouth was full of nails, I knew what he'd really meant to say was I could be anything at all so long as I didn't call myself born-again. He didn't want me to fool myself, to replace intelligent thought with blind faith. So when I came upon Christianity during my own adolescent journey of discovery, with plenty of exposure to all the religious and lifestyle alternatives, it was the worst kind of rebellion in Dad's eyes. He figured I'd dabble in drugs like other teenagers or have too many boyfriends for my own good, not that I'd find solace and truth in the only thing he could never make sense of.

But those red words in the Bible spilled and stained like they were written in blood, and Christ-love began to replace my childish (mis)understanding of dragons and matzah and confession and religious extremism. Bible pages became roof thatches as I hid beneath their cover and rebelled against my very upbringing there, where I found solace from alcoholism and algebra, divorce and acne and the aches and wounds of teenage relationships, and, later, from my own bad and brief marriage when I was still a child and they were my ribs being broken for the sake of a love that wasn't really love at all.

The words gave me strength to see beyond the injustices of a world I couldn't understand, and I ate them up, devouring every bite, and they sat in my belly and sustained me. They sifted, for me, the difference between what was and what shouldn't be and what love and life and living *could* be. Page by page, proverb by parable, I moved from simply ingesting those words and cowering beneath them to chewing and internalizing and eventually overflowing with them until they poured out of my very own fingers, an offering back to Christ, a rent payment for the room and board of all these years. Like Fulghum and like the disciples and like Jesus himself, I'm learning to use words in a vastly expansive playing field—the sameness and difference of human experience, the space where worlds collide and we connect and crave the words of intimate understanding in the middle of our hungry lives, and we all bite in and it drips from our chins…

We are what we eat.

Likewise, I'm learning to dig in and extract my worth from the concrete words of Scripture that tell me who I am, not in checks and balances, in failures and successes, but in grace and promise for the girl in the mirror, worth far more than nonsense and nothingness; worth the sacrifice of the Word-Made-Flesh, even. I'm thankful for the word-feast I've enjoyed, a bountiful banquet of classics and essays and Scripture, and for the Word of God in particular, the only words to satisfy my voracious hunger; this Word alone, my bread. And if the Word is my bread, oh, that it would be true that I am what I eat, indeed, and that I would always have a healthy appetite for what sustains.

From Under a Bonnet to Freedom

Janet Oberholtzer

Our intense game of dodgeball is interrupted by a call to dinner. My cousins and I are hungry, so we stop the game knowing we'll play again after the meal.

We noisily file into the house already filled with dozens of aunts, uncles, and other cousins. The kitchen counter is crowded with serving dishes filled with familiar Pennsylvania Dutch food. An extension table surrounded by chairs stretches through the kitchen into the adjoining living room.

Adults claim the chairs at one end of the table while cousins fill in the remaining seats. After a silent group prayer, the steaming platters are handed to the man of the house sitting at the head of the table. He serves himself before passing the dishes around the table.

I'm starving and I can't wait to get back to our game — but instead of being able to eat and chat with most of my fellow dodgeball players, I stand by watching them.

My extended family is too large to all eat a family-style meal at one time, so we eat in shifts. The normal practice is for the men and boys to eat first and the women and girls to serve them. After the males finish eating, the men find comfortable chairs in the parlor and the boys return to the dodgeball game.

Before the women can eat, we wash the plates, silverware, and cups. (No one has a dishwasher, and paper products are never used for family dinners.) After the table is reset, the serving dishes are retrieved from the oven, where they were put to keep the food warm.

The women in my family are a fun, lively bunch and we chat as we eat, but half of my mind is on the dodgeball game happening without me. I eat then sneak back out to the game, hoping no one notices so I'm not called back to help with the dishes.

This was life in my world in 1975 and I accepted this type of thing as normal because not only did I see it in my family, but I also saw it in many different scenarios within the strict Mennonite sect I grew up in. All the leaders of the church were men. All the school board members were men. All the major rules of church, school, and home were made by men.

The principle that men were the leaders and women were the followers was taught by example and by words at home and at church. There were also many spoken and unspoken rules about what was acceptable or not for women.

Not only was there a difference in the gender roles, there was also a vast divide in the dress restrictions. The men's wardrobes had progressed almost at the same pace as the rest of society's. They had similar haircuts and, other than the oldest generation, most wore jeans and tee shirts.

On the other hand, women's dress restrictions hadn't changed much since the late 1800s. We were forbidden to cut our hair. I had long pigtails until age fifteen, when I had to start wearing my hair pulled back into a bun with an uncomfortable head covering over it. I had to wear long homemade dresses — whether working in the barn, playing dodgeball, or ice-skating on the neighbor's pond. But the whole idea that dresses were more modest than pants didn't work out so well during a walk-on-my-hands phase I went through around age nine.

The church leaders, who enforced the rules, frustrated me, but they insisted it was "God's ordained way for mankind." This caused me to view God as a harsh dictator with a grudge against women. It's no surprise that I wrestled with my worth as a girl.

I'd lie under the stars at night wondering why I was born a girl and why God was so unfair to girls and women. I tried to imagine how great life would be if I'd been born a boy: Not only would I have more fun and more privileges, but I would have more value as a person.

At first, I wanted to be a boy simply because I gravitated to the outdoors and to things that were considered boys' activities. With time, the wrestling moved to an intellectual contradiction that was hard to reconcile. I couldn't understand why many people and, supposedly, God viewed men and women so differently. Why were certain things acceptable for men but not for women? And why was one gender the leader of the other if we were all created equal?

As older teens, my friends and I pushed our boundaries and went bowling and roller skating and hung out with people outside our church community. During those times, I was frustrated with how the boys blended into society with ease while we girls were often subject to uncomfortable looks of curiosity because we looked like we'd just stepped off the Mayflower.

As I looked ahead to my life, it was depressing to think that I would have to fill the expected roles for women in looks and actions. When I wasn't outdoors, I was the kid with her nose in a book with secret dreams of being a writer someday. But I didn't think that could happen because I didn't know of any women writers in my culture.

So I became a person divided. Part of me wanted to ignore all those cultural rules and roles, but the principles were engrained in me so strongly that I couldn't just shake them off. They hounded me and I vacillated between trying to be myself and trying to mold myself into a woman who would be respected in my family and the church community. The division in my soul left me feeling insecure and worthless. Tears wet my pillow more nights than not as I tried to figure out who I was and what I was worth.

I wasn't really sure I wanted to get married or have children, but I dated in my teen years because marriage was what all Mennonite girls wanted. After not being impressed with the half-dozen guys I dated by the age of seventeen, I decided I'd swear them off for a solid year.

That lasted about two months — then I met Jerry.

Jerry grew up in the same Mennonite sect as I did, but he was different from the other guys I knew. I couldn't quite put my finger on what was different, but I liked it. With time, I discovered it was that he valued me (and all women) as a person with equal worth to his.

We followed the model we were surrounded with by marrying young at 20 and having three boys over the next few years. But during our early years of marriage, we left the strict Mennonite sect and attended a local church, which had roots in the Mennonite community but had moved away from its religious tradition and identified itself as non-denominational.

I embraced the new freedoms I now had: fashion, hairstyles, and entertainment choices. I also appreciated the broader view our new church offered concerning gender roles. Though women were encouraged to be at home if they had young children, it was acceptable for a woman to have a job outside the home or to continue her education.

That church went through various phases over the next decade, ranging from fundamental to slightly charismatic to seeker-friendly to evangelical with a touch of reformed. But throughout all the changes, one thing stayed consistent: Only men were in church leadership, and the church taught the concept that "men are the head of the household." I've never wanted to be in church leadership, but I was baffled at this boundary they insisted on keeping about gender roles. Yet I resigned myself to the idea that if the good people of that church saw men and women as equal in everything except church leadership and head of household, then apparently that was where the line was drawn and I needed to accept it.

So even though it didn't make sense to me, I did accept it. Because of the harsh view of God I developed growing up, I lived with an unhealthy fear of him, so I thought in order to please him, I had no choice but to believe what the church taught. And deep within my psyche, my insecurities still told me that since I was a woman, I didn't have the same worth as a man. I assumed there was something wrong with me because I couldn't reconcile the contradiction: Though God had different roles for men and women, it shouldn't affect the worth I felt as a woman. I kept thinking if I stayed the course long enough, maybe it would eventually make sense.

Jerry never wavered from his view that men and women had equal worth and equal right to choose any path in life. Whenever I brought up the subject (again) he'd remind me that having a vagina didn't change my worth as a person or limit my choices.

Life was busy with our boys, a business, and too many bills, so there was little energy left for me. I drifted along until my thirties, when I discovered running. Running strengthened not only my body, but also my mind and spirit. It helped me gain confidence to sort through my confused beliefs about my own worth. The gap in my mindset about the differences between men's and women's worth decreased. I became more comfortable with myself.

But my journey toward self-acceptance was rudely interrupted at age thirty-eight when I almost died in a six-vehicle accident. I hovered between life and death for forty-eight hours and then spent four years recovering from my injuries and then from the depression that followed. This crisis sent me into an emotional and spiritual hurricane and some of the progress I had made in discovering my own worth evaporated. I was back to some former defaults — feeling insecure and worthless. Life seemed pointless and, for a few scary months, I struggled to find a reason to live.

Only with counseling and allowing myself to go through a major renewal did I learn to live again. I came to see that my confusion about God and my worth (or lack thereof) in his eyes was one of the reasons for my depression. So I quit God as I knew him and, as much as was possible, started over with a clean slate. I allowed myself to explore every mindset I had about God and humanity.

I researched, read, and asked questions. I sat and thought — and thought some more. Sometimes moving forward involves looking backward. I remembered how much I enjoyed being outdoors as a child, so I spent hours in nature absorbing the warm sun and the fresh air. My injuries prevented me from running for four years, but I knew being active always made me feel alive, so I went for walks and I bought a kayak. Spending hours paddling on my local lake was healing, and I discovered a new sense of wellness.

I went from seeing God as a harsh dictator with a set of rules that I needed to decipher correctly to follow to seeing God as love. I went from seeing Jesus as someone who was my ticket to heaven to being a teacher of this love. I saw in his stories that a life well lived is one where more focus is put on interacting with others in a kind, loving way than on religious traditions.

I went from seeing people as men or women with differing values and specified roles to seeing people as unique individuals each having equal worth and the precious gift of choosing what path to take in life. I went from doubting my own worth to learning to love myself for who I am—not in a narcissistic way, but in a healthy way.

Though my insecurities still trip me up at times, I now know that I am a person of worth, not based on my gender or anything I've done—but simply because I am.

Speaking Worth Without Words

Beth Hall

It seems that women will constantly be assigned value from men — fathers, boyfriends, sons, brothers, bosses. We are hesitant to assign worth to ourselves, afraid we might be arrogant or cocky. And to assign value to another female implies, at least on some plane of our psyche, that we have a say-so in the allocation of worth and are somehow more important than the woman in question. But I only understand the nonsense behind these attitudes because of my own journey to true and biblical self-worth, which is due in no small part to a group of men: my Christian brothers.

As a college freshman, I had a boyfriend who was not a believer, and his ideas about womanhood and beauty were far from biblical. My choice to dress simply and modestly — partly out of habit and partly out of insecurity, not at all from spiritual conviction — did not please him. He would say things like, "You never dress up for me" or, "Why don't you try to be prettier?" I never felt good enough to have him love me, and I constantly felt put down in some way or another.

Despite this relationship, I was hungry for God. I joined a Pentecostal college ministry and was soon immersed in a community of believers who were going after the Lord with all they had. Part of that pursuit of Jesus meant a deep respect and protection of non-romantic heterosexual relationships. Brotherhood and sisterhood were important, and my friends and peers were working hard to maintain those relationships purely and wonderfully. We pursued friendships with one another, we encouraged each other in our faith, and, most important for my journey to self-worth, we valued each other in concrete ways.

On the road to a state-wide retreat in a car full of tired but excited college students, I got a call from my mom. We were talking about the next morning and how I was planning to skip my shower and makeup, which to me was a sacred morning ritual, so I could get another half hour of sleep. Then, came a moment I will never forget as long as I live.

I said to my mom, "I'll be in a better mood even though I won't be a very beautiful sight to behold."

From the driver's seat, I heard, "Yes, you will. As a Christian woman, you will." My brother in Christ stated this just as matter-of-factly as he would have said that the sky was blue or that it was 7:30 p.m. There was no question or pause in his voice, just the declaration of beauty in the body and soul of a woman who praises the Lord. And my heart heard, "You are beloved."

This concrete valuing of one another did not just happen in random moments, though. It was a lifestyle. Some of us girls would jokingly commiserate about a certain guy in our group who was especially protective of his Christian sisters. At any time past 10 p.m., we were not allowed to walk the two blocks from the library to our dorms by ourselves if we had been studying anywhere near him. Although it was annoying at times, when it came down to it, none of us would trade the attention and priority he gave to us, ensuring that his sisters were okay. Walking home alongside a godly man not only assured me of my safety, but it showed me that I was cherished — and by a man with no agenda or romantic interest in me. I learned that romantic interest was not a prerequisite to chivalrous treatment, and my heart heard, "You are prized and esteemed by the Father — and by others."

Later, I was in a season of intense gratitude. God had pulled me out of the muck of my relationship, and I was literally singing His praises. I was also running out of worship music that I knew. So on a fairly consistent basis, I would ask our student worship leader about the lyrics to songs that moved me during weekly services. Faithfully, he emailed me lyrics to songs along with encouraging words. "Sing your heart out before the Lord!" he would say. And my heart would hear, "You are lovely. Your worship of the Most

High God is valuable to the Lord and beautiful before His people."
By giving his attention, his time, and his efforts to strengthening me
as a worshipper, he gave that worship value. My friend affirmed
my worth not just as a woman, but as a worshipper.

My Christian brothers were invaluable along my journey to true
self-worth. But my final step away from insecurity and toward
self-worth was the most important one because it started with both
a man and a woman. One of the couples that pastors my college
ministry has several small children, and they asked me to babysit
for them. I said yes, and a couple days later I was on their living
room floor, laughing and playing with three beautiful kids. A mom
and a dad had entrusted me with their most precious possessions.
Being trusted this way by people of both sexes was more than my
worthless self-image could take, and I finally started to see myself
as truly valuable.

As a woman, as a life-giver, I gave of myself to this family and
thereby to the ministry that had so blessed me. I was able to give
something concrete—time and, in a round-about way, money. (I
babysat for free. Getting paid never entered my mind.) I was able
to contribute something to their lives that had, at the most basic
level, a monetary value. Because of me, they did not have to pay
a babysitter so they could have a date night as husband and wife,
and their children were well cared for and loved. My gift to this
family was a cold, hard fact, and even if my heart wanted to reject
the truth behind my brothers' actions, it could not reject this. In my
own abilities, I was contributing to the success of a family—my
insecurity couldn't touch that.

My ex-boyfriend's hurtful expectations slowly faded from my
heart and were replaced by godly truth from Christian brothers
who showed me my worth rather than reminding me of my faults.
These brothers were for me and our other sisters, for us to have an
intimate knowledge of ourselves as valuable, beautiful beings. And
my pastors' trust revealed to me just how valuable I was to God's
kingdom—just how much worth I had on a grand scale.

They all spoke loudly with their actions. When I didn't have to
open the door for myself, I heard, "You are beautiful." When
I didn't fear for my safety walking home, I heard, "You are a
treasure." When I didn't have to stand alone in grief or pain but
was lifted up in prayer by my brothers and sisters, I heard, "You

are valuable." And when I was trusted with my friends' beautiful children, I heard, "You are worthy."

None of us, male or female, can assign worth to another. But with our actions, we can speak affirmation of true worth into others' hearts even if sometimes we don't speak at all.

Declare and Release

Janae Maslowski

I have never been comfortable with the beginning. Eden. Woman damning all. With a beginning like that, I am distilled down to this: Born female, my life is an apology. I must endlessly show I am other-than-Eve. I must prove I am of worth. To beg-pardon for being a girl, I limit my body, my emotions, and my opinions. I learn quickly how to gain approval. I increase my attentiveness, likeability, responsibility and busyness. Quick and efficient, I decrease my sexuality, intellect, creativity and presence.

I explode, a volcano. Forged in the womb, a self never fully sealed, I was made to shift and evolve, to ebb and flow. I am dangerous. Steadfast is safe, but my plates always collide—I erupt, molten me spewing through. I try and I try. Oh, She knows I try. But I don't understand at 7-years-young why I can't be quiet like my sister and contained like my brother. I sit in my red fury, confused, alone, afraid of my strength, lost in the midst of organic, volcanic me. I determine I will organize. I will keep the looks at bay. I creep quietly over to her, this volcanic self; I'm armed with a tool to silence, and I don't let up til she stops kicking.

I go to sleep counting food. Success and failure are one breath apart. Each day is forever; scales can be tipped at any moment, nightmare unending. The only relief is to consolidate. In loathing of my curving edges, I shame myself into taking up less space. My body demands food; I deny the need. I'm determined. There won't be anything left for people to judge, disapprove of, control. But though I live in extreme, I can't win. My curves are etched into my mind and I cannot starve my mind out of seeing round.

I am blank. So long as I live empty, myself locked away, I am safe. I learn the womanly arts of waiting, reading body language, stroking egos, and avoiding conflict. I am groomed for pleasing and I do it well. As I improve in these fine arts, I am praised and hailed as leader, to be watched, a kingdom-builder. They see their smiling poster child, but inside I am a fury; I am becoming a revolutionary with *Fuck!* scrawled on the wall.

I try to speak. My words, a jumbled mess, fall from my tongue. I am called a verbal-processor; all I know is I am desperate. If someone doesn't hear me, declare me okay, I cannot be free. I will be trapped forever in my crazy, begging relief, a drop of water in the midst of my hell. So I don't stop; I fight. I'm not sure I live, but I sure as hell fight. And I can't stop, because what if the answer is no? What if Jesus stops advocating for women before the Church leaders finally listen? What if I am meant to remain beholden to all, lost to myself? What if I am just plain crazy? Another woman, woven into the Larger, dying for a life that I cannot have.

I exist in duality. Outside I am ever the no-needs female; I give in excess and then give to gone, which is praised. I work out my repentance in London, a year-long volunteer, street wanderer. I hide from carbs and conversation; Starbucks, my sanctuary; running, my salvation. Under no uncertain terms I deny myself and serve others. I am dying for lack of care. Inside, I am full of fierce explosions; I am Guy Fawkes, won't stop til Parliament is blown to hell. In secret, I map out my spiritual independence day. But you'd never know because I champion the loudest for that which I hate. I have no choice. I am the Church's property. My friend, who carried me in her womb and carries me now, arrives at Heathrow. We wander cobblestones; I talk to exhaustion. I am walking dead with lava burning through my veins. There is nothing left of me to take. In this vast bleak and burn I find the courage to speak my anguish, my secret: *I am being used by the Church — I am its whore. Why doesn't anyone stop this abuse?* I name the black; I dissolve.

I am perfect. I've perfected perfection. Regardless, the noose tightens — I am one breath away, one misstep and I hang. But I won't mess anything up; it is not an option. Perfection is my survival, not my salvation—I cannot be saved. There is no end; I've been set-up. God is male. I am female; I am lost.

I ignore the skipped over, the blaring, the obvious. I pretend I can relate to a bearded man in the distant blue. I act as if it is perfectly normal to always say He and never She. As if it doesn't slight me and limit me, a she. I speak of His love, ever His good and faithful little girl. I say He is accessible, approachable, relatable. I deny that I want to live in my body, my female self, because I know where the power lies. It is His, and therefore it is in possession of the he's and never the she's. More than wanting power, I yearn to trust myself. Eden burns my chest with crimson shame, reminding me that I cannot trust myself. I am female after all.

I dream of living next to the surf, a free spirit, sexy, strong, alive. My God, but I want to live in my skin. That isn't possible. My skin is dangerous and not to be trusted; I am to deny my flesh in order to serve, love, and give. I am to accept my role as deceiver and come under the covering of men who will protect me from myself. It is best to move from father to husband.

I wake up in a cold sweat. I fear my husband will be sandal-wearing, Bible-pounding, me-deleting. I'm London drowned, raging inside. I meet him—he offers me a smoke. I feel safe that he isn't good. Over coffee and brilliance we break bread. I rage out loud and I swear in excess. I won't let him think for one moment that I am predictable, controllable, usable. I dare him to just try and force me to think like him, to be as I am not. For all my blind rage, he remains. For all my fear, he is love.

I am betrayed. My body, life-drunk, lost to all else but creating, supporting, and expanding. My body, declaring me woman. I, the stillborn soul, am growing a life and I don't like it one bit. I've fought for thirty years to consolidate, to not take up space, to be pleasing, organized, androgynous, a zero. Now I am being called out, made to go public.

I am opened. The babe is born and I emerge holding his heel. I am Jacob to his Esau. I am bleeding, won't stop; I am told to look at my child, to behold my son. I don't know how to connect—I am lost to myself. The life is draining out of me; for all of my forcing, I cannot control it. Finally, I look to my son, my living; I kiss his forehead and my body releases his encasing.

I encounter myself. Met by my Forever, I come undone. The eternal flame is in my bones; the chaff of my life burns hot, fire cleansing til only ash remains. I am reduced down to Now. I am a monk with babe in arms. We rise at all hours to chant our salvation; our breathing, a prayer. Planted deep in black, Moon declares me her daughter, a cycling being who grows to give and then gives to gone. As I am broken and given for his living, I try to speak, to utter gratitude. Into the dark I fling my trust, in hope that I will be heard. Through our communion I am brought to low, I am brought to ask. I am empty, I am need.

I am saved through my living. I am met by my Savior in the midst of the forcing, the hiding, the bleeding, the giving, the needing, the loving, and the dying. I am not carried quickly away from the pain; I become acquainted with myself in the dark. I learn black is sister to light. That life is no larger than a breath. That it is always a matter of letting go and letting go. That life is Now. That I must die and die and die, for there is no other way to live. And I want to live. I am a woman, a self, a daughter of the Divine She, He, and Neither. I am found woven into the Larger, connected by deep female roots, Eve living in us all.

Whose Mirror Is It?

Diana R.G. Trautwein

Lilly is 22 months old and a real pistol—funny, charming, inquisitive, secure in herself and in the love of her family. She plays with us two days each week, one of the perks of grandparenting and retirement. And every time she's here, I celebrate who she is becoming.

Last week, she climbed up onto my bed (where all good computer work is done in this house) and begged to see "pichures, pichures!" So I opened iPhoto and went directly to her favorite event: her older sister's sixth birthday party. Each time we look at this set, we scroll through all 90 photos, identifying as many people as we can, usually lingering longest at the pictures of the "happy cake-cake."

Lilly has not quite grasped the truth that these "pichures" she loves so much are only two-dimensional representations and not actually tiny versions of the people she sees every day. Sometimes she will cup her hands next to the screen and say, "I pick her up! I pick her up!" puzzled that she can't quite make that happen.

But one day last week, she surprised me with words that marked my heart in a powerful way. She surprised me with what she *did* understand. She saw a close-up of her own face, and she patted the screen gently, saying, "Oooh, that's Rirry [still working on those L's]. She so cute. I ruv her."

Oooh, that's Lilly. She's so cute. I love her. I wrapped my arms around her small body and kissed her on the back of the neck and said, "Oh, *yes*, Lilly. You are so cute and I love you, too. I hope and I pray that you will always be able to look at yourself in exactly this way. Always."

What is it that happens to us between early childhood and adulthood? Why is it so easy for us to lose that clear, common-sense, of-course-I'm-loveable-it's-just-so-obvious-I'm sure-you-can-see-this-too sense of our value, our worth, our intrinsic rightness? And what—as parents, aunts and uncles, siblings, cousins, grandparents of girls—what can we do to foster an atmosphere in which little girls will always see themselves this way? When we look in the mirror at age 16 or 21 or 35 or 50 or 75 or 90, why shouldn't we be able to see ourselves through eyes of love?

Is this not the message of the Gospel? Is this not the truth that Jesus saw and taught and modeled and lived: That fundamentally, to be a human person is a good, good thing? So good that God chose to be clothed with our flesh, to walk through the steps of our life, to eat and sleep and laugh and cry, to connect with others and to spend time alone, to hang out with all different kinds of people and see each of them as interesting and important and valuable? Yes, I think so.

Oh, but what about how messed up we are? How crazy, mixed-up we are? How broken and battered and bewildered we are? Yes, indeed, we are all—male and female—flawed, in need of rescue, standing in the need of prayer, called to repentance. We are fallen and we are broken. And realizing that we are sinners is a powerful and important part of our personal development and our spiritual journey. But—*but*—our sin is not the most important thing about us. Our created humanity is.

One of the saddest things about the dominant teaching of most of the western Protestant Church for the last few hundred years is that we have lost sight of this foundational truth. Jesus came because God loves us; God views us as worth the cost; God sees in every one of us a prize of inestimable value, sin and all. In truth, God chooses to see *through* the sin and the brokenness to the treasure that waits within.

So, the story of salvation has one over-arching purpose: to restore to us the fullness of God's design. We are, every one of us, image-bearers, carrying the imprint of the Creator from the moment of our conception. And my not-quite-two-year-old granddaughter has caught a glimpse of this truth, whether she fully understands it or not. She looks at herself and says, "Yes!" just as she is; she offers a rousing "amen" to God's good creation. She looked into the "mirror" of my computer screen last week and she saw the truth.

What if we could gently guide our girls—and ourselves—to look into that kind of mirror, a mirror that tells the Truth? Because most of the time, I do believe we're looking into exactly the wrong mirror.

Maybe we're looking into the mirror that our parents used, the one that warps things a little. Our mother's mirror that worries we won't be pretty enough, or thin enough, or popular enough. Or our father's mirror that worries we won't be ballsy enough, or smart enough, or strong enough.

Or we're looking into the mirror that our culture puts up in front of us, the one with all the lights around the edges, the one that screams, "Look like *her*. Don't look like you. Look like that tall, skinny one over there, the one that's been air-brushed to the point of no longer looking remotely like a member of the species."

Or sometimes, we're looking into the mirror that a particular kind of church holds up and waves menacingly in our face. The one that growls, "Beware of letting your beauty show too much—you might tempt someone into sin." Or, "Look like everybody else here, please. Matchy-matchy!"

So here's what I would like to suggest. Let's show the girls in our lives the mirror that reflects who they truly are. Hold it up—the one that speaks the good words from the Good Book—and speak to every one of them the truth:

See? You are delightful, a wonder; you are one-of-a-kind, irreplaceable; you a gift, a creature filled with glory! Do you see this person? She is lovely—just because she *is*. Not because of what she adds or subtracts; not because of what she does or doesn't do; not because she cleans up her act or morphs herself into someone she isn't, but because of *who she is*: a daughter of the Most High God, uniquely created, finely crafted, generously gifted. And *loved*.

Conclusion

I had been hard at work for months on a book I thought everyone else needed, but with each page it was becoming painfully evident that I was a physician in need of healing myself. And as I grew increasingly aware of the myriad and profound ways the world had altered the views I and so many others had of ourselves, I became a mother on a mission, intent on building my children up at every opportunity.

"How did you get to be so lovely?" I asked my two-year old girl.

"Because God made me," she said. And it was so simple to her, so matter-of-fact, that I beamed for the joy of the truth my daughter held; and I ached to know I'd lost it.

I thought about my dearest relationships, my proudest achievements, my talents, my beauty — the foundations on which I'd built my life, my worth, myself. And I wondered: If I lost it all, if one day I lay disfigured and disabled and disowned, if the only contribution I could make to the world was my breath, would I still be worth anything?

I realized that the only way the answer to that question could be yes was if my worth were an intrinsic part of me. It could not be manufactured or manipulated; it could not be earned or lost. If I had any true and enduring worth, it had to have been woven into my being from the start.

Then I thought of my child, who was woven together inside of me. I thought of why I loved her, not because of any act or quality of hers but simply because she was mine. And I began to believe in the truth that she knew. My essence was found in being God's child. I was woven and wanted and made full of worth.

The question was answered even before I was born.

About the Authors

Part 1: Relationships

Pilar Elvira Wolfsteller- The Wedding Bouquet

Pilar Elvira Wolfsteller is a journalist who spent the past two decades living and working in Europe and the Middle East. For more than 15 years she was a writer, editor and television producer for global news organizations that had her covering everything from stock markets to summit meetings to sports extravaganzas to war zones. In 2006 she shifted her focus to corporate communications and now specializes in social responsibility, sustainability and ethical business issues. She flies small airplanes and writes non-fiction for fun.

Chrystal Westbrook Southwell- Lesson Learned: The Handicap of Being Born Female

For more than 20 years Chrystal Westbrook Southwell juggled two full-time roles, as an executive in a professional services firm, and as an associate pastor in a Pentecostal denomination. This experience has given her unique opportunities to see how women are perceived within different kinds of organizations and cultures. She married her college sweetheart after a 25-year delay (it's a long story) and moved to Toronto, where she's still a bit shaky on the rules for hockey, but has enthusiastically embraced the wonder of gravy on french fries. Read more from Chrystal at life-after-church. com.

Alise D. Wright- The Distance Between

Alise Wright is a wife, mother, friend, musician, and writer, but most of all, she is a woman in progress. She has edited Not Alone: Stories of Living with Depression and Not Afraid: Stories of

Confronting Fear both with Civitas Press. You can read more of her writing at knittingsoul.wordpress.com.

Merritt Onsa- Being Set Free

In 2001, Jesus stepped in and flipped Merritt's world upside down. Ever since, she longs to live her life trusting in God's grace. Merritt and Todd were married in 2009; shortly after, she started a blog at livesimplylove.com in which she tackles the realities of marriage and handling conflict with love and humility. A professional writer, Merritt uses her talent to help nonprofits share their story in order to raise money and do good in the world. Today, she and Todd reside in Colorado where they regularly marvel at the beauty of God's creation just outside their front door.

Renee Ronika-Winter

Renee Ronika, a university English instructor, commits to honest faith and bold vulnerability as a writer, speaker, event coordinator, and minister. She ushers others into the same healing rooms of God that she visited during her own journey toward overcoming. She publishes poetry, non-fiction, and fiction; in 2010, her short story "Fathers" received an honorable mention from *Glimmer Train Press*. Renee resides with her husband and their two young daughters in the Wild West—her hometown of Phoenix, Arizona—where she's discovered green grass and true community after fifteen years of living abroad and throughout the country. Read what's on her mind at quietanthem.com.

Jennifer Luitwieler- On Belonging

Jennifer Luitwieler writes about faith, family and running at her site, jenniferluitwieler.com. Her first book, *Run With Me: An Accidental Runner and the Power of Poo*, was published in September, 2011 (Civitas Press). She is a Pittsburgh transplant who, after nearly 18 years in Tulsa, OK, still clings to her Ohio Valley roots, though each of her three children are Okies, born and bred. She and her husband homeschool two of the three and run their fall weekends by the Pittsburgh Steelers schedule. Find her on Twitter, @jenluit, or Facebook, Author Jennifer Luitwieler.

Part 2: Abuse

Julia Lunardo- Out of Misery and into Joy

Julia considers her family her most precious blessing in life. She enjoys doing sudoku puzzles, reading, exercising, and entertaining, and has great appreciation for music, dance, and theatre. She has a tender heart for children, and is thankful for the talent God gave her for teaching. She has owned and operated a dance and music studio for twenty-seven years and is also a high school Spanish teacher. Julia is deeply grateful for the gift of faith which has sustained her through darkness and opened the door to joy. Having survived childhood sexual violation as well as domestic abuse as an adult, and having experienced the awesome love of God she can tell you this:

You deserve joy
You always have
Because you are His
Beautiful creation

Alex- Who Told You That You Were Naked?

I'm not Alex anymore. I use my old "working" name here to protect my daughter. There may come a time when she wants to know the details of my former life, but until then, I protect her from finding them out by any other source but myself.

It has taken decades of struggle, but God has gifted me with a celibate life and much healing. The scars remain, but they fuel my passion for rescuing and loving other victims of this broken world, especially those who have experienced the horrors of human trafficking.

Love is the answer to it all.

Shanda Sargent- Of Tears and Healing

Shanda Sargent belongs to her beloved, Matt, and homeschools their four crazy-amazing kids in the foothills of the Rockies. After leaving 20 years of professional ministry, their family recently moved across the country and is "ruthlessly trusting" God in the midst of plan B.   Shanda blogs at theupsidedownpastorswife. blogspot.com, where she transparently shares her heart's ramblings about life and grace.

Janet Heath- The Unwanted

Janet Heath is an avid reader and movie aficionado. Her greatest wish was to be a movie/book critic growing up, but the realities of life got in the way. She loves a good romance novel but lately has a growing affection for vampires (the modern kind!) and watching The Walking Dead. Her most favorite books of all are the *Earth Children* series by Jean Auel. She lives in a vacation wonderland on The Chain O' Lakes in Antioch, IL with her fur kids and writes the occasional blog at janheath1234.wordpress.com.

E.L. Farris- Reckoning Day

E.L. Farris, a born-again Christian, ex-lawyer, runner, and married mother of three children resides near Washington, D.C. She is the author of Ripple, A Tale of Hope and Redemption and I Run: Running from Hell with El. Prominent in her work is the theme of women helping women thrive and find healing despite difficult circumstances.

Sarah Moon- I Am Human

Sarah Moon is a feminist, a Unitarian Universalist, a geek, and a Women's and Gender Studies student. She is interested in the intersections of feminism and faith and is currently researching the way that Christian cultures handle violence against women. Sarah blogs about her journey of healing from abuse and fundamentalism at SarahOverTheMoon.com.

Part 3: Society & Culture

Marilyn Gardner- Relentless Pursuit

Marilyn Gardner is a nurse currently living in Cambridge, Massachusetts. She loves God, her family, and her passport (in that order). Marilyn grew up in Pakistan where the Call to Prayer was her alarm clock, curry her favorite food, and veiled women her friends and surrogate aunties. As an adult she has lived and worked internationally as well as on the east coast, the west coast, and points in between. She blogs at Communicating Across Boundaries about life, faith, travel, third-culture kid peculiarities, cross-cultural communication, Pakistan, the Middle East and more.

Jennifer Deibel- The Real Me

Jen is your typical American wife and mother living life, raising kids, and working; only she's doing it in Ireland. She is married to the love of her life, Seth, and is extremely blessed to be mom to two delightful little girls and one hilarious little man. Jen passionately loves the Lord, her family, music, dance, writing, coffee and chocolate (not always in that order). She writes at This Gal's Journey and is a monthly contributor at The Better Mom.

Deborah Bryan- Patchwork Umbrellas

Deborah Bryan is a writer hailing from the Pacific Northwest and, not coincidentally, now living in Long Beach, California. She is the author of several novels, exactly one of which she has managed to edit. In between mothering and negotiating contracts, she is working on more writing and editing projects than she can count, and loving every minute of it.

Alexandra Rosas- Blessed to Be a Woman

Alexandra is a first-generation American who writes memoir and humor for various writing websites. She posts on her blog Good Day, Regular People of life in a small town as the mother of three boys where she tries hard to go unnoticed. She was named a 2011 BlogHer Voice of The Year for Humor, a 2012 Babble Top 100 Mom Blogger, and 2012 Most Interesting Blogger and Best Female Blogger by Studio30Plus, an online writing community. She was part of the nationally acclaimed The Moth Live Storyteller's Tour, and is currently seeking a publisher for her memoir *Just Visiting. The Real Story of Milwaukee's First Latino Gang: Tales of an immigrant family and their Colombian bandana-wearing ways.*

Idelette McVicker- Brokenness: Our Perfect Equal Sign

My name is Idelette (pronounced Ee-de-lette) and I would like to go to every country on the earth to meet our world's women. Meanwhile, I get to learn about Love and living out justice with sisters from all over the world as founder and editor-in-chief of shelovesmagazine.com. I also work part-time with NightShift Street Ministries in my city.

I was born and raised in South Africa. Then I spent a good chunk of my formative twenties in Taiwan before I flew across the Pacific to start a new life in Vancouver, Canada. Here I pledged my heart to Scott 13 years ago. We have three children (9, 7 and 5) and I live by the Chinese proverb: When sleeping women wake, mountains move.

Give me some sweet chai, vanilla rooibos or pearl milk tea and I'm in heaven. And if you don't know this about me quite yet: Jesus is my hero.

Melody J. Wachsmuth- The Secret of a Woman

Melody J. Wachsmuth is a freelance writer and mission researcher based in Osijek, Croatia. As she travels through the Balkans, she searches for true stories that can inform, encourage, and challenge people. She loves learning about cultures, adventuring in the wilderness, and listening to people's stories—and revels in the rare moments when all three of those elements come together. She shares some of the stories on her blog: balkanvoices.wordpress.com.

Part 4: Expectations & Pressures

Renée Schuls-Jacobson- Work Makes Whole and Holy

The mother to one teenaged son, Renée A. Schuls-Jacobson scribbles ideas for essays on scraps of paper and then loses them. Red-hot momma or red-hot mess (depending on the day of the week), she is the girl with the big hair and the big ideas. And the words.

Stephanie S. Smith- Mary, Muscle of Love

Stephanie is a writer and editor generally addicted to print and pixels, and fascinated by the Incarnation and matters of embodied faith. She has worked for RELEVANT Media Group, Barna Group, and now serves as associate acquisitions editor at Zondervan in Grand Rapids, Michigan where she lives with her husband. You can find her at www.stephaniessmith.com or tweeting @ stephindialogue.

Amy Nabors- Good Enough

Amy is a southern girl born and raised in Alabama where she lives with her husband and son. A part time photographer, she also spends her days painting, serving at her church, and blogging at ordinarilyextraordinary.com where she shares her photography, art, and thoughts on faith. She tries to see the extraordinary in an ordinary life as she discovers her voice and art through a journey of faith and grace.

Lindsay Holifield - The Weight of Shame

Lindsay is an artist and student at the University of North Texas.

Kara Gause- Private Lessons

Kara Gause is Yankee girl who fell hard for a Southern musician and now finds her feet (happily) planted in Nashville, Tenn. A former actor and educator, these days you will find her wrangling their twin preschoolers and (hopefully) writing.

Sarah Bessey- A Letter to My Daughters

Sarah Bessey is the author of "Jesus Feminist" (Howard Books) and an award-winning blogger at www.sarahbessey.com. She lives in Abbotsford, British Columbia with her husband and their three tinies.

Part 5: Faith & Church

Anne Bogel- (Not) One of the Boys

Anne Bogel is a writer who lives in Louisville, Kentucky with her husband and four kids. She blogs at Modern Mrs Darcy, where she addresses timeless women's issues from a timely perspective. Anne is a graduate of Wheaton College, where she studied Christian Education.

Cara Sexton- The Sustenance of Words

Cara Sexton is a mom of four who lives in Ashland, Oregon, where she tries not to notice that she's the oldest freshman on the university campus. She blogs at whimsysmitten.com and dreams ridiculous dreams with the support of her amazing and hilarious family. Look for her book, *Soul Bare*, releasing in 2013 by Civitas Press.

Janet Oberholtzer- From Under a Bonnet to Freedom

Janet likes good food, dark chocolate, and fine wine; thankfully she also enjoys running. In the past, along with being called a tomboy and a troublemaker, Janet has been called a gardener, seamstress, event organizer and business owner. Today she works as a writer and speaker. Her first book, Because I Can: Doing what I can, with what I have, where I am was released in 2011. It's a body-mind-spirit memoir about her journey from waking up in a hospital to discover she might never walk again to completing two marathons.

Beth Hall- Speaking Worth Without Words

Beth Hall is a joyful college grad who lives in Knoxville, Tennessee, roots for the Vols all day long, and seeks to glorify the Lord through honest worship and deep, compassionate relationships with others. She loves to quilt, read, write, and sing, and thinks a great cup of chai or coffee on her front porch is the best companion to the Bible. She enjoys hiking in the Smoky Mountains, visiting family and friends all across the country, and live music. Beth is also an alumna of and long-time volunteer with Hugh O'Brian Youth Leadership. She can be reached at bethhall20@gmail.com.

Janae Maslowski- Declare and Release

Janae was born of deep waters, into a world of flow and magic. Right/wrong and either/or started to replace her embodiment. Into the heavens she went, to protect herself from the confines of religion. The rigors of perfection took hold, although life continued to bubble within and break through her resolve. Janae is eternally grateful that Love slayed her through the birth of her son. She is still trying to welcome the grounding of herself into body and Now.

Janae makes home with her husband in Oregon. They are welcoming a second child into their family.

Diana R.G. Trautwein- Whose Mirror Is It?

By the grace of God, Diana has managed to live a lot of interesting lives. While a student at UCLA, she married at twenty. Two months after graduation, she traveled to Africa by freighter, brought home a baby two years later, had two more and stayed home to raise them for twenty years. A whole new career in ministry began in her 50's. Now a certified Spiritual Director and a regular blogger at dianatrautwein.com, she continues to encourage women to look in God's good mirror as she meets with people one-on-one in her small study and as she listens to them online. Lilly is now almost three and still thinks she's pretty darn cute.

Made in the USA
Charleston, SC
26 March 2014